Successful Endurance Riding

**Patricia Ingram
Lewis Hollander**

The Stephen Greene Press
BRATTLEBORO, VERMONT

Produced in the UNITED STATES OF AMERICA.
Designed by DOUGLAS KUBACH.
Published by THE STEPHEN GREENE PRESS, Fessenden Road, Brattleboro, Vermont 05301.

FRONTISPIECE PHOTO: This Tennessee Walker mare, a refugee from the show ring, loves covering the country. Endurance riding is a great sport for you if you are interested in truly being one with your horse—and a genuine horseman.

Library of Congress Cataloging in Publication Data

INGRAM, PATRICIA, 1956–
    Successful endurance riding.

    Bibliography: p. 185
    Includes index.

    1. Endurance riding (Horsemanship)   I. Hollander,
Lewis, 1930–   joint author.   II. Title.
SF296.E5I53   798.2′3   80-28784
ISBN 0-8289-0423-5

*This is for all
the good horses
in the world.*

Contents

Foreword

by Sharon Saare

ENDURANCE RIDING is a great and fast growing sport not only in this country, but throughout the world. Participating in rides means many things to many people, and certainly of major value is the opportunity to see and ride through new country on a well-conditioned, healthy horse.

One factor common to all rides is 'the trail'. Without trails there can't be rides, nor, equally as important, a place to prepare for them.

In the early days of endurance riding, access to trails was far less of a problem than today, simply because fewer people were involved in other kinds of outdoor recreation. Along with a continually increasing population, other demands for access to the kind of country we enjoy (and must retain entrance to if our sport is to flourish) increase.

Today's land-use policies are to a large extent determined by how many use what and in what way. Therefore horsemen—trail riders—must stand up and be counted, must become actively involved to assure that they receive consideration when the recreational land-use pie is divided.

Becoming active in trail preservation may appear to be far removed from actual endurance riding—perhaps because trails you are using now are as yet unthreatened. But, remember that every trail already lost to horsemen was at an earlier time unthreatened; that as suburbia continues to sprawl, open spaces—previously available to all of us—become contested, and often closed, one by one.

What can you do about trail preservation? First and foremost, trail riders must realize that they are responsible for the protection of their own interests. No one else is. It will be up to you to respond to issues affecting you. Don't assume 'someone else' will take care of it—you are that someone. Become involved with your local State Horse Councils, State Horsemen's Associations, and particularly Trails Councils. Be sure your activity is represented.

Throughout the nation, major planning projects are now underway in every state. These planning efforts will continue for some time and they are establishing land-use policies that will affect all horsemen for years to come. Take the initiative. Find out what is happening in your state, your county, your city. Check into planning that will affect horsekeeping and horse use of trails. Make certain that the decisions being made now will not effectively phase out our activity—endurance riding—so dear to all of us.

Be encouraged to know that when endurance riders have made the effort, the results have been most favorable. In spite of development, trail corridors and horse use of them have survived and can survive in your area. You too, can make a valuable contribution to trails preservation.

Good riding and good luck!

ACKNOWLEDGMENTS

We would like to thank the American Endurance Ride Conference and the riders of the Pacific Northwest Endurance Riders; Jackie Grape; Heidi Smith; Neel and Lucille Glass; the American Bashkir Curly Registry; Susan Gibson and "Trail Blazer"; the Appaloosa Horse Club; Winkie and Matthew Mackay-Smith; *Equus* Magazine; Boyd and Karyne Zontelli; Pat and Holly Gervais; and Mark Ingram for all their help.

ILLUSTRATION CREDITS

Frontispiece, Mike Campbell; *p. 5*, Jimmy Butler; *p. 14*, courtesy the Appaloosa Horse Club; *p. 15*, courtesy the Appaloosa Horse Club; *p. 17*, Mark Ingram; *pp. 18–19*, courtesy the Appaloosa Horse Club; *p. 25*, courtesy Bashkir Curly Registry; *p. 29*, Hollander; *p. 31*, Ingram; *p. 32* Sharon Saare; *p. 41*, Ingram; *p. 44*, courtesy Neel and Lucille Glass; *p. 45*, courtesy Neel and Lucille Glass; *p. 56* (top and bottom), Jerilyn Freimuth; *p. 59* (top and bottom), Jerilyn Freimuth; *p. 60*, Diane Jones; *p. 66*, Hollander; *p. 71*, Jimmy Butler; *p. 73*, Mike Campbell; *p. 80*, Diane Jones; *p. 97*, Jerilyn Freimuth; *p. 102*, courtesy Pat Gervais; *p. 103*, courtesy Boyd Zontelli; *p. 104*, courtesy *Western Horseman* magazine; *p. 115*, courtesy Lewis Hollander; *p. 121*, courtesy Boyd Zontelli; *p. 123*, Hollander; *p. 125*, Diane Jones; *p. 140*, courtesy Pat Gervais; *p. 149*, Nancy Springer; *p. 155*, Jimmy Butler; *p. 161* (top) courtesy Lewis Hollander; *p. 161* (bottom), Nancy Springer; *p. 162*, Nancy Springer; *p. 166*, Jerilyn Freimuth; *p. 171*, Jerilyn Freimuth.

Successful Endurance Riding

Introduction

WHEN LEW AND I first discussed doing a book on endurance riding, we realized there were two major aspects to be covered.

First was the basic tenet of endurance riding: *To complete is to win.* That's what makes the entire sport possible and attractive.

The second was *winning* endurance rides, one of the toughest challenges in horsemanship. It's not for everyone, or every horse, but part of this book is written for those that aren't content with less. You may not always win, but you feel a lot better when you've had a good try. The only time this gets out of hand is when you risk your horse in a foolish effort and fail even to complete the ride.

We found that the books on endurance didn't cover the aspect of winning very thoroughly, so this one came into being to answer all the questions that we had asked when we first started out.

Lew and his wife Hanne have been devoted endurance riders for many years, and I have been following the sport for several years. Our views differ, but there's room for different opinions in a big sport like endurance. After you've competed in a few rides, you'll have opinions of your own.

Lew's contributions deal with what it takes to win from a scientific point of view; I concentrated on building the foundation of a good endurance horse.

Through the years Lew has evolved a set of basic principles that express the tone of the book. These "rules" have worked well for many top competitors, especially in the Northwest region, home of four national champions so far, and more just waiting for a chance.

The biggest contribution endurance can make is a kinship between you and your horse from the long hours of training and competition. In an age when many horses spend most of their hours stabled and under a trainer's care, endurance stands out as a do-it-yourself sport. You don't need years of lessons and several thousand dollars in tack to compete; all you need is a little persistence and a good horse.

Know your horse and accept that you are a member of a team, not a passenger. The *trail* is your adversary, not other riders. Completion is really the goal, and winning merely icing on the cake. You must be totally committed to helping your horse in every possible way. This means being in good enough physical condition to help him on the trail. When you can make faster or equal time on foot, do so. As the rider, you are expendable physically, but you are also the brains of the outfit. Strategy is your concern, as is the care of your horse. This includes preparing for the vet stops out on the trail, before arrival, and never passing up a chance to offer your horse a drink unless the finish line is in sight. It also means preparing for the next race the very moment that you cross the present finish line.

Endurance riding has come a long way from the early years, and it can go much further. For such a young sport, it has done remarkably well. Some of the topics in this book may become outdated in future years, or considerably advanced, but this is a start.

1: To Complete Is to Win

ENDURANCE RIDING is defined as an athletic event in which the same horse and rider cover a measured course of 50 miles or more within a maximum period of time.

The first horse to finish in acceptable condition is the winner, but each and every finisher is a winner, too, because he completed the ride. The challenge in endurance riding is the doing, as well as the winning. Whether it takes three hours or nine, everyone that crosses the finish line can be credited with a major achievement.

Endurance rides are open to every horseman with a sound horse of any breed or sex. The horses must be a minimum of five years old and pass a thorough veterinary inspection before and during each ride.

Specialized equipment is not needed to get started in endurance riding. Experience and miles soon teach the endurance rider what will work best.

THE ESSENTIAL QUALITIES

The most essential qualities in an endurance rider are determination and persistence. Endurance is not an easy sport, but a rewarding one in terms of accomplishment. There are no large purses or fantastic awards. Most of the time there is only a buckle or a piece of tack to remember the ride by. The important award is the completed miles. A horse and rider can accumulate miles together for year-end awards. Several riders have over 5,000 miles, and there are horses with more than 3,000 miles in competition.

Not every horse is capable of finishing an endurance ride, or continuing on to such high mileage totals. An average horse quits when he gets tired. A good horse goes on as long as you ask him to. A great horse goes on to win.

It's not easy. Sometimes you have to carry on when you're extremely uncomfortable. Perhaps your nose is sunburnt, or you've got blisters where you never thought you would get them, but you finish what you started. Regardless of the discomforts, endurance riding is fun. It's like marathon running. The sense of accomplishment makes it all worthwhile.

There are other benefits. You will find that many experienced riders are willing to help you through a ride with whatever is required—advice, encouragement, or assistance. They'll loan you equipment, feed and horse liniment. Their pit crews will give you a drink of water, a sandwich and a chance to wash your face. If you lose a shoe, someone will get you back on the road with four again. If you have problems of any sort, someone will help, even if it slows them down. And you will be everlastingly grateful to the horseman who held his fresh horse back to keep your tired horse going.

The other riders in your region will become a large, extended family. If you catch a severe case of "Endurance Fever," you may find yourself living a gypsy life, going from ride to ride, craving miles the way a dieter craves chocolate sundaes. It becomes a pleasant habit, wearisome at times, but rewarding when you cross the line for the very first time, and every time after that.

ENDURANCE HIGHLIGHTS

Endurance requires true horsemanship. It is possible to be a flawless equitation rider, but know little of the horse. It takes a great deal of skill and judgment to ride a horse many long miles in a single day without harming him, and leaving him fit to ride another day. You'll become one with your horse. Riding will be instinctive, and you'll know exactly how your horse feels. In return, your horse will develop a great deal of personality because he gets so much loving attention. You will learn to trust him in a crisis, and in turn, he'll trust you.

There are 50-, 100-, and 150-mile endurance rides. Some have required rest stops; others allow you to choose your own rest periods as long as your horse is doing well. Stop and go rides are becoming popular because they are easier on the horse, though they do demand more rider strategy.

In a stop-and-go ride, veterinarians monitor the horse's condition at various points throughout the course. The horse may continue only after his pulse and respiration drop to an acceptable level.

You are allowed 12 hours to complete a 50-mile ride, and 24 hours for a 100-miler. The 150-mile rides vary in time allowances, depending on the difficulty of the terrain.

A horse may be withdrawn at any time by either the rider or the veterinarians if he is worn-out, lame, or just not feeling right. Protecting the horse is the primary concern of everyone in endurance riding.

Long-term accomplishments are treasured more than a single win. The rider who never makes the top ten, but completes every ride, may find himself high in the year-end standings with total mileage. This sport rewards the tortoises as well as the hares.

There's a place for everyone in endurance riding, whether junior, senior, lightweight, heavyweight, or pit crew. There are kids on lead lines, retired folks, and people from every occupation out there on horseback.

A LITTLE HISTORY

Originally, endurance rides were put on by military groups and were often uncontrolled. A typical long-distance cavalry race in Europe would result in dead or useless horses.

The United States Mounted Service Cup was inaugurated in 1919, and the trial consisted of 60 miles daily for five days on the roads of Vermont and Massachusetts. The United States Cavalry carefully policed the participants to protect the horses. They wanted to determine what horses were best for cavalry purposes, and how to travel long distances without harming the horses. Specifications read that the distance must be covered in not less than 10 hours daily, and not more than 12 hours, and that each horse had to carry 200 pounds. Points were given for speed, low feed consumption and condition; the overall aim was to determine what made the best cavalry mount.

*Ramla, a Crabbet Arabian import, won the first ride in 51 hours and 26 minutes, followed by purebred and part Arabians.

The 1920 ride was won by a Thoroughbred, Mlle. Denise, in 46 hours and 59 minutes, with other Thoroughbreds and Arabians following. The weight requirements were stepped up to 245 pounds per horse.

Paved roads between Red Bank, New Jersey, and Washington, D.C., comprised the 1921 ride, and only seven of seventeen entries finished, with the purebred Arabian Crabbet winning. Crabbet finished the ride in 49 hours and 4 minutes, followed by Rustem Bey, a part-Arab that had been a consistent competitor throughout all of the rides.

The 1922 ride shifted emphasis to speed and was held at Fort Ethan Allen, Vermont, with 21 horses competing. The Thoroughbred Vendetta won in 45 hours and 17 minutes. No Arabs placed high in the standings.

The last ride was held in Avon, New York, in 1923 and was won handily by an Anglo-Arabian, Gouya, in 45 hours. Rides held after this one were not interested in endurance, but true speed.

The first modern endurance ride was put on by Wendell Robie in 1955. He selected a trail first used by pioneers and the Pony Express between Lake Tahoe and Auburn, California. Robie called his ride the Western States 100 Miles One Day Ride, and for many years, it was the only endurance ride in the world. Also known as the Tevis, it is now one of the largest rides, and a Tevis buckle commands respect in endurance circles, for the Tevis trail is one of the toughest anywhere.

The American Endurance Ride Conference was organized in 1971 to promote endurance riding by distributing information and keeping trails open to horsemen. AERC sanctions rides in the United States and compiles points for every horse and rider that participates in recognized rides.

AERC also established the ground rules for endurance rides, which follow.

The first horse to finish (in the least amount of time) in acceptable condition is the winner.

There shall be an award available for the best-conditioned horse.

There shall be no minimum time limit.

The ride must be controlled by the veterinarians.

Every finisher will receive a completion award.

Endurance rides are open to all breeds of horses.

Rides must be a minimum of 50 miles long the first day.

The American Endurance Ride Conference maintains permanent records of all horses and riders for historic and informational purposes. They encourage better horse care and prevention of cruelty to animals.

Today there are rides throughout the world, the offspring of the Western States Ride, and thousands of endurance riders.

Perhaps the sport of endurance riding flourishes because "The outside of a horse is good for the inside of a man."

2: An Endurance Horse Is an Individual

IT'S NOT HARD to find a horse able to complete an endurance ride; the difficulty lies in finding one with the stamina and soundness to continue competing year after year, preferably in the top ten or twenty finishers.

WHAT TO LOOK FOR

Soundness is the most important point to bear in mind when shopping for your new endurance prospect, or when looking over the horses you now own. Any weakness of conformation will make the horse more injury-prone, or less efficient in covering the miles.

Type is the next consideration, for you want a horse that will work for a living. He may not be as beautiful as the show horse, but he'll go all day and all night if he has to.

Most endurance horses are small and wiry, without excessive muscling. This means less meat to pack around, and that the horse will shed heat better. However, the rider's size must also be considered, since a heavyweight rider needs a horse big enough to carry him if he plans to compete hard. Otherwise, he'll have to plan on doing a lot of running.

A wiry horse is trim with long, smooth muscles. Horse muscle tissue consists of three different types of fibers, each performing different tasks. They are fast twitch, high oxidative fibers; the slow twitch fibers; and fast twitch fibers.

Fast-twitch fibers produce intensive speed for short periods of time, such as sprint races, and make up the bulky, bunchy muscles.

Fast-twitch, high-oxidative fibers can be trained to do either slow or fast work. Endurance horses have a high proportion of these

The size of the rider should be in proportion to the size of the horse, but it's not a hard and fast rule. This Arabian mare carried a heavyweight rider 50 miles in just under 9 hours, but he did a lot of walking on foot.

and the slow-twitch fibers that can rest and refuel themselves without stopping, as long as the effort is not excessive. The long slender design of the fast-twitch, high-oxidative fibers produces longer strides because they can stretch further. Longer strides mean fewer are necessary, and the horse gets a quick rest in between strides.

The more slow-twitch fibers a horse has, the better suited he is to distance work. These fibers were studied by Australians, Drs. David Snow and Reuben Rose. Their research compared biopsies of muscle tissue from different types of horses. They discovered that the amount of slow-twitch fibers varied from one breed to another, with Arabians averaging highest, along with a Thoroughbred cross. Slow-twitch fibers do mundane chores, like keeping the horse on his feet; they obtain their energy from oxygen.

A moving horse generates part of his motion with a slingshot effect using rebound from stretched muscles. Weight is placed on a foot and the pastern sinks down, stretching the muscles and tendons to their limits. The horse travels forward and takes the weight off of the foot, getting almost a trampoline effect to boost him along. That's why long muscles give a horse a mechanical advantage.

Where the Energy Comes From

It takes energy to make your horse go, and there are two ways for the muscle fiber to get it. Oxygen is used in the *aerobic* process, which is the most efficient. Aerobically, the fiber can get nine times the amount of energy obtained anaerobically, without tiring, and could go on indefinitely if oxygen and energy were unlimited. Each fiber would be ready to go immediately, over and over, in slow work.

The *anaerobic* method, producing energy without oxygen, is wasteful and produces the by-product lactic acid. When the horse can't get sufficient oxygen to keep going, such as at a fast gallop, the muscle fibers are running on anaerobic energy. The resulting lactic acid causes problems by interfering with the electrolytes, turning the blood acidic and sometimes damaging muscles. As the acid accumulates, the horse finds it painful and begins to tire. At that point, he needs to rest and repay the oxygen debt that he has incurred. The circulatory system just can't keep up with the oxygen demand at high speeds.

Fast-twitch, high-oxidative fibers can learn to produce energy both ways, depending on demand. This means that you can go long and slow, which is what the majority of endurance riders do, or fast and then rest when the horse needs it.

It also means that the horse that looks like a body-builder's dream is not a good endurance prospect. He's probably muscle-bound and uncomfortable to ride. Save him for chasing calves in an arena.

Don't go too far in the opposite direction, however, and choose a gazelle-type without substance and bone under him. You aren't looking for coarse bone like a draft horse, but for something that can take a lot of concussion.

The endurance horse should have the overall look of an athlete, moving freely. Watch him as he moves around in a corral or pasture. Does he skim the ground or pound like a cart horse? If he pounds, both you and the animal are going to take the brunt of it. Size doesn't necessarily mean much when determining whether a horse moves well. Some big horses float over the ground.

You are looking for a horse that moves economically, with a hunter-type stride, not a flashy park style. If you are looking at gaited horses, chose the one that has the longest, plainest stride. Action is pretty, but it can really take a lot of energy out of the horse—energy that could move him forward instead of up. Also avoid a choppy, pony stride.

Size-wise, most endurance horses average 14 to 15 hands, and weigh anywhere from 850 to 1,050 pounds. There are larger horses that do well, but they are the exception rather than the rule.

Now that you've watched the horse move, get back about ten feet and study his conformation. Look for balance and symmetry. He should appear rugged but not coarse, with a deep heart girth. A shallow-bodied horse lacks stamina and may be a hard keeper as as well. Horses that have been raced usually have excellent heart and lung development to match the deep chest. If they retired sound, they make a very good prospect.

Don't worry about appearance unless the horse is so ugly that you couldn't stand to live with him. It does no good to have a beautiful horse that quits ten miles from the finish line.

This George Phippen sketch of the ideal Appaloosa also shows the ideal endurance horse. This might look like an Indian cayuse to some, but has desirable traits in a horse expected to cover lots of miles. The horse is small, wiry and tough-looking; just the kind to accept a challenge. An Arabian would have some differences in conformation, such as a flatter croup, but the basic requirements hold true.

THE FINE POINTS

Get close to the horse and study him in detail, starting with the head. A horse uses his head for balance, and it should be in proportion to the rest of his body. The eyes should be large and clear and seem quiet. The horse that looks cranky may be a pretty good fellow, but a friendly face is associated with a better disposition. The nasal cavities and nostrils should be large. Desert Arabs used to slit the nostrils of their warhorses to allow more air to reach the lungs.

A wide forehead, large nostrils and intelligent eyes usually indicate a horse that will be pleasant to work with. The animal should appear alert and curious about his surroundings, but he need not be too spirited. The best horses learn to save energy for when it's needed.

The neck should be trim, not coated with heavy layers of muscle or fat. You can certainly take the fat off, but it's easier to start with a correct neck, preferably with an arch over the crest, not ewed. These points have more to do with appearance than with endurance ability, but if you are interested in other events, such as dressage, keep it in mind.

The shoulder should have a good slope of approximately 45 degrees. This increases potential length of stride and makes gaits smoother, as well as running effects of concussion. Remember, a

These are the front and rear views of the ideal Appaloosa as visualized by Phippen. The chest of the ideal endurance horse should be a little wider for good lung capacity. Notice the straight legs with good-sized hooves that are in proportion to the rest of the horse.

rough horse pounds himself just as hard as he does the rider, and it doesn't do him any good.

The legs must be straight and travel cleanly. A farrier can correct many problems, but it's easier to start with a good traveler in the first place. The pastern angle should come close to matching the angle of the shoulder. Too straight means rough gaits, and too sloping means potential weakness or even an existing injury. The pastern angle should carry smoothly through to the foot, with the wall of the toe matching the angle closely.

Short, strong cannon bones are an indication of strong legs, and long forearms make a long stride possible. Look at the legs for interference marks and old injuries that could bother him under stress. If he's not traveling cleanly now, he'll cut himself to pieces after 50 or 100 miles. If interference problems are due to poor shoeing, a common cause, you can correct them. If conformation is the cause, remember that excessive corrective shoeing can cause future problems because of the stress involved.

Your endurance horse is going to need good feet. If he doesn't have them now, you can improve them over a period of two years, but that's a long time to wait when you only have one horse. The foot should have a good, strong wall with a thick sole. If there are already hoof cracks and a crumbling, shelly wall, you're going to have a tough time keeping shoes on him.

Four black hooves are ideal, since white walls seem to crumble and break easier. They must be in proportion to the horse's size. Beware of the big horse with teacup-sized feet. These feet are going to pound hundreds of thousands of times in conditioning and competition, and they have to be able to take the shock.

Your endurance horse needs good withers and a short, strong back. There are successful long-backed horses, but they're not the best for carrying weight for long periods of time. If the croup is higher than the withers, your saddle will be pushed ahead, possibly soring the back. If the back is swayed, the saddle won't fit correctly; it will rest on the withers and loin like a bridge over a gully.

This half-Arabian mare is a perfect example of a horse totally unsuited for endurance riding. She is overweight with heavy muscling, and her straight shoulders give her a rough, short stride. Her withers are also very poor, being wide and flat instead of well defined.

Before you make your final decision on buying an endurance horse, have a veterinarian give him a complete check. The vet can't guarantee that the horse will stay sound forever, but he can point out potential problems, and determine whether existing blemishes, such as splints, could cause future problems because of severity or location. If the horse is an experienced endurance horse, he could be for sale because he's burnt out and used up. A veterinarian will help keep you from buying someone else's wind-broken problem.

Important points in the conformation of the legs and hooves

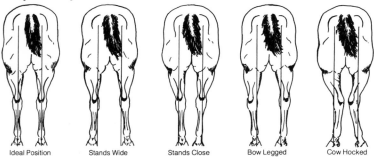

Ideal Position   Stands Wide   Stands Close   Bow Legged   Cow Hocked

Vertical line from point of buttock should fall in center of hock, cannon, pastern and foot.

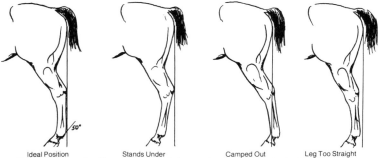

Ideal Position   Stands Under   Camped Out   Leg Too Straight

Vertical line from point of buttock should touch the rear edge of cannon from hock to fetlock and meet the ground behind the heel.

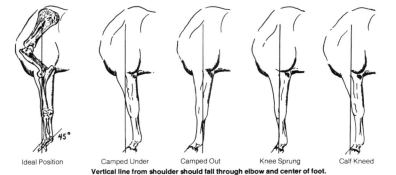

Ideal Position   Camped Under   Camped Out   Knee Sprung   Calf Kneed

Vertical line from shoulder should fall through elbow and center of foot.

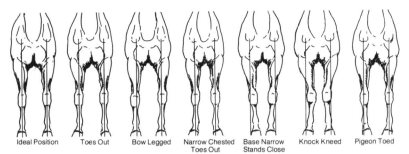

| Ideal Position | Toes Out | Bow Legged | Narrow Chested Toes Out | Base Narrow Stands Close | Knock Kneed | Pigeon Toed |

Vertical line from point of shoulder should fall in center of knee, cannon, pastern, and foot.

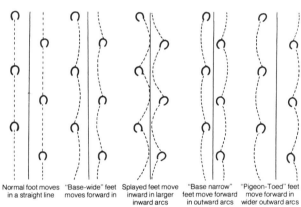

| Normal foot moves in a straight line | "Base-wide" feet moves forward in | Splayed feet move inward in larger inward arcs | "Base narrow" feet move forward in outward arcs | "Pigeon-Toed" feet move forward in wider outward arcs |

Path of the feet as seen from above

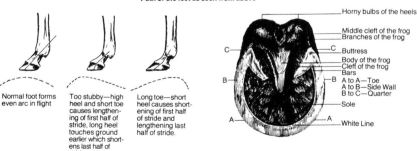

Normal foot forms even arc in flight

Too stubby—high heel and short toe causes lengthening of first half of stride, long heel touches ground earlier which shortens last half of stride.

Long toe—short heel causes shortening of first half of stride and lengthening last half of stride.

Horny bulbs of the heels
Middle cleft of the frog
Branches of the frog
C—Buttress
Body of the frog
Cleft of the frog
Bars
A to A—Toe
A to B—Side Wall
B to C—Quarter
Sole
White Line

THE ACID TEST

If the horse is of riding age, try him out under saddle. Is he easy to handle, or is he half-rocket? A hot-tempered horse can be difficult to handle in crowds, impossible to rate, and prone to nervous problems and colic. However, he's easier to ride than the horse with absolutely no impulsion. A middle-of-the-road horse is ideal, particularly for the novice. It can be devastating to drag a lazy horse 15 miles.

A good walk is essential. If he walks like a turtle, you're going to have to ride that much harder to make up time lost. The trot should be brisk, not draggy, with good impulsion. The horse should travel with some natural collection, not dragging his rear-end around behind himself. You can train him to travel well, but it's much easier to start with a good, efficient mover in the first place. The canter is the least important gait for most riders. It is used primarily as an alternate gate for variety. Some horses travel more efficiently and comfortably at that gait than at a fast trot. If you're looking for a top-ten horse, he will have to be capable of covering long distances at the canter or hard gallop.

Courage and desire are absolutely necessary. The horse must be willing to go forward, always forward, whatever the trail. Just like any other athlete, after all the strategy has been used, and all of the energy spent, the rest of the race is run on heart alone. You don't want a horse that quits when he feels tired.

Psychologically, a dominant horse will often do better than a passive, herd-bound animal that wilts under a challenge. The horse must be capable of working alone, or in a crowd, and be able to take care of himself without being a troublemaker.

A gelding is the best all-around competitive horse because he hasn't got anything else on his mind. Mares and stallions will have value in future breeding programs, but they tend to be more emotional and unreliable. The high-hormone levels in mares and stallions might be an advantage, but it is too often wasted in "social" behavior the night before. A gelding is also quieter and less likely to cause problems, both in hauling and at home in the corral.

If a breeding program is part of your future plans, study the bloodlines of the mares and stallions you consider. Bloodlines in a gelding can indicate potential ability and aptitude, just as in other horses, but they aren't useful for future generations.

If you are looking at young colts for races far in the future, breeding will be the main indication of potential. It's not easy to determine what they'll look like when they grow up, but if the dam was a thousand-miler and the stallion a champion, you can hope strongly for a winner.

Don't ever make the mistake of breeding a mare, or a stallion for that matter, that has proven unsound for the task at hand. That's just perpetuating problems for future generations.

A stallion is for the experienced rider only, because he reacts to other horses and his surroundings much more than the gelding or mare, and can be difficult to handle around mares in heat. Don't dream of rambling the hills on your beautiful black stallion unless you know you can control him.

MATURITY IS IMPORTANT

Age is another consideration, for a horse must be at least five years old to compete in rides that are 50 or more miles long. Ideally, the horse should be at least seven or eight, for maturity improves the horse and strengthens him. Some endurance horses don't reach their full potential until 8 or 9, after they've gone 1,000 miles in competition.

Racing hard takes a great deal out of a horse; maturity seems to make it easier on him. The upper limits of age are harder to define. There are horses in their late teens capable of completing carefully paced races, and some in their early teens that are tough competitors. Horses with a lot of experience can teach you a lot about the sport.

Color is something to think about, but not one of the things that will make or break you. Gray or light-colored horses will tend to reflect some heat; dark horses absorb it readily but cool down more quickly. One of the principles of thermodynamics is that darker surfaces radiate heat more readily, so a dark horse will cool down faster under the stresses of racing. But most people don't worry about that. Lew favors grays, even though physics doesn't.

An endurance horse has to be an easy keeper and a good eater. He'll be working hard, and eating is the only way he can replenish himself. His body must be efficient at converting feed into energy. If he eats and drinks well on the road, there won't be worries about how well he'll do after refusing to eat or drink for two days.

Your endurance prospect should have a low resting pulse and show potential for fast recoveries when conditioned. A low pulse indicates an efficient heart that pumps a maximum amount of blood at each beat, referred to as maximum minute-volume. When working, you want the heart to pump the utmost amount of blood at each beat, and at the fastest possible beat. Minute-volume refers to the amount of blood moved in one minute. The more moved, the faster you can ride, because it helps protect the horse from fatigue and keeps him going longer.

The horse has to be efficient, not only in his physiology, but in his way of going. After a certain point, a lengthened stride takes too much effort to be sustained efficiently. More strides per minute become the most effective way to cover country. An efficient mover will also be easier on his own body in terms of concussion and stress. The leg travel patterns should be straight and clean, as any tendency to brush or interfere will increase with fatigue, possibly causing severe injury.

WHAT ABOUT BREEDS?

Arabians dominate the endurance trails, but many other breeds are also successful. An endurance horse is an individual, not yet a breed, and it is impossible to generalize by saying that every member of a certain breed can or can't do a certain job.

The 1978 national champion was a Thoroughbred–Quarter Horse cross, and another Quarter Horse was reserve champion some years back. Appaloosas have done well, and Morgans are making their mark. The Morgan gelding, Caballero, set a mileage record in 1979 with 1,700 miles in 26 rides. Mules are also capable of many miles as shown by Deacon, who did 1,200 miles in 1977.

In distances over 50 miles Arabians are generally superior, particularly in racing situations. Supposedly, desert sheiks ran their stallions until only one survived, then used that one for the basis

Table 1
ENDURANCE SUCCESSFUL BREEDS

In the first seven years of endurance riding as organized by the AERC, the following breeds achieved top-25 honors in national standings. A total of 152 horses were honored from 1972 to 1979.

Arabian	105
Grade	27
Appaloosa	6
Morgan	4
Thoroughbred	3
Quarter Horse	2
Pinto	1
Buckskin	1
Mule	1
Paint	1
Pony of the Americas	1

Many of these horses have a large percentage of Arabian blood, although not all are registered. Nine horses have received three or more best condition awards in a single year; eight were Arabian and one was a grade horse.

of a breeding program. Contemporary Arabians have changed a great deal since then, and some lines have lost their distance ability. The Polish lines and some Egyptian families are the best, since they haven't been bred exclusively for looks. The Polish horses always had to earn their papers on the race track; this guaranteed that those Arabians could perform under stress. Indiscriminate breeding and automatic registration of colts has taken its toll since.

You must decide if you wish to complete rides comfortably or race. A gaited horse like a Tennessee Walker or a Saddlebred can be very comfortable, since they were bred to be smooth and durable under saddle. Don't confuse the abused show ring stock with the trail horses. Many gaited horses have never seen a show ring, or had their feet messed up, and they are excellent prospects. You can also try to salvage a spoiled ring horse for trail riding, but you will be starting with a disadvantage.

Any light-framed, good moving horse can be competitive. The "distance models" of Appaloosas, Quarter Horses and Morgans can do well, but you must choose carefully, going back to the working type. Some of them are only capable of going in circles, slowly, and you don't want that! The Indian type of Appaloosa can be especially tough, and the same applies to cowponies and the original Morgans. Stay away from excessive stockiness and heavy muscling, though.

Don't ignore the rare breeds, such as Bashkir Curlies. Some of these unusual breeds have exceptional endurance characteristics and are quite tough. There are far too many breeds to discuss each one individually.

If you already have a horse and you like his breed, well, give it a try. There are Thoroughbreds and many, many other breeds placing regularly and completing consistently.

This is also a sport where grade horses can be outstanding. Kathy Golis picked Smokey, an Arabian–Standardbred cross, from a group of horses destined for the cannery. Smokey won his second National Junior Championship at the age of 12.

Jay's Curly Boy is definitely a horse of a different curl. Ridden by Shanna York and owned by Jay McKendry, both of Morgan Hill, California, this gelding is registered in four registries. He is a member of the Bashkir Curly, Appaloosa Horse Club, International Arabian Horse Association, and Endurance Horse registries.

Another interesting type is the Moyle horse, developed by the Moyle family of Star, Idaho. They are large, rugged horses that tower over most of the other endurance horses, but keep right up with them. They show a draft influence in their heads and feet, but move lightly and beautifully. A good Moyle might be an excellent three-day-event prospect for someone who was interested in both eventing and endurance, as the breed is similar in type to the Hanoverian. Some Moyles show "Dragon Points," bony protuberances over the eye, just small bony bumps that don't affect them at all.

If you can't afford to pay a lot for a horse, and are willing to accept a challenge, consider adopting a young mustang. Many have a lot of Thoroughbred in their background, along with draft, and are tough little guys. Most have excellent bone and some are beautiful movers. You must start with a young colt, however, and take very good care of it so that it fulfills its genetic potential. A four- or five-year-old mustang has put up with a lot of short groceries and illnesses, and probably will be stunted. If you go this route, choose them at the corrals from the main herd, not from someone's second pickings, and take someone with you that knows how to choose horses in the rough.

EARLY TRAINING IS IMPORTANT

The Hollanders have developed a ten-year program for building highly competitive endurance horses. They buy prospects as colts, and raise them just the way they want them raised, with lots of handling and good care. They prefer starting with ranch-bred horses that are growing up on pasture and range land. The first years are critical in forming good legs, heart, and lungs. And they prefer prospects related to other successful horses. The young horses are broken to saddle at age five and then, for the next year or so, begin to learn what it's all about. A lightweight rider will take them through their first endurance rides when they are six or seven years old, and at seven or eight, they begin racing to win. The horses are allowed to mature completely before being asked to work.

The Hollanders do their horse shopping at the Hyannis Cattle Company and Rushcreek Ranches, where many good Arabians come from. Many of the great horses of the sport are Nebraska-breds.

The initial cost is a minor point, since there is so much spent in training and time to develop an endurance horse. The Hollanders feel that cost isn't too significant if the horse looks like a winner, with breeding and conformation as indicators.

Another place to consider looking for endurance prospects is the track. Horses that were too slow, or otherwise unsuited to racing, but are sound, can make good endurance horses. You'll find they're pretty hot to handle for the first few rides, and you may prefer to go with a quieter horse that wastes less energy going straight up.

Whichever horse you choose, keep in mind that you will be asking a lot from the horse, and spending a lot of time with him. Shouldn't you at least be friends?

3: Building a Winner

BEFORE THE WORK of conditioning begins, you have to lay a foundation of good health care, feeding and shoeing. You also have to decide what type of tack to use, whether to make do with what you have, or re-equip for a new sport.

EQUIPMENT

On the subject of equipment, there is no need for expensive, fancy tack. Good quality tack that is well designed and correctly made will last many years if cleaned and cared for properly. Junk, on the other hand, will have to be replaced every year until you learn better.

Choosing a Saddle

Starting with saddles, there is a wide range of choices; previous riding experience will be a factor. Lightweight stock saddles, English jumping and dressage saddles, and the specialized endurance saddles are all suited for the purpose. If weight is a concern, the English and McClellan saddles, plus a few endurance saddles, are the lightest and fit a wide range of horses. There are risks, though, particularly when you buy a bargain saddle that isn't stout enough to take the beating. The risk is to your horse's back, and perhaps to yourself when the saddle disintegrates.

You must decide just how interested you are in this sport and other equine competitions. If you think this might be a passing fad, or you've been riding western all your life and don't know if that postage-stamp saddle will hold you up, then you should start with a sound used saddle, preferably of good quality.

English saddles are the most common on the trail, and can be fitted to almost any horse. An all-purpose model is best, since an

Hanne Hollander poses Law Thunder after a win in the Sunriver 100. She is riding a Stubben dressage saddle and using a mechanical hackamore with a roping rein and a tailing rein. The tailing rein is light cord that makes it easy to dismount and run with the horse while keeping him under control. A breast collar completes the outfit. Not one bit of unnecessary weight is carried.

extreme forward-set style doesn't protect your legs when you are riding with long stirrup leathers. Dressage saddles put your weight in an excellent position for the convenience of the horse, and a deep seated one will make the converted cowboy feel more at ease. The park saddle is not designed for lengthy rides and places a rider's weight on the horse's kidney area. That adds up to problems you don't need.

The best English saddles for trail use are the Stubbens, a Swiss saddle styled with a deep seat and sturdy tree. They can be a large investment, since used saddles can start at $400 or more, but you'll get your money out of it if you decide to sell it in the future. Good saddles appreciate in value, and a good Stubben lasts 20 years or longer.

You can try an inexpensive Argentine saddle if you are uncertain about English saddles; this will let you find out whether this style will work for you or not. It won't cost much, but after about a year of hard riding, you will have to take it out behind the barn and shoot it—the tree will probably be broken by then or damaged beyond repair. Cheap saddles cannot take the constant pounding of posting mile after mile.

If you are considering a western saddle, it must have a balanced or forward seat, as found in the Monte Foreman saddles, allowing you to sit over the center of gravity. Stirrups must be free-swinging, so that you may stand in them and maintain your balance easily. The saddle should be as light as possible. Rigging should not be double, but three-quarter or other to prevent galling. The double rigging was made for roping, and as a compromise for less skilled construction and design. You may want to condition in a heavy saddle and compete in a light English or endurance saddle.

Special endurance saddles are designed on a lighter tree and have no horn. This allows you to get well forward without being impaled. Some are made with additional padding to protect the horse and the rider. The models are constantly changing, so you may want to see what stands the test of time before rushing right out to buy one.

The original endurance saddle is the United States Army McClellan, consisting of little more than a tree with stirrups and cinch. It is light and has an open back, allowing excellent air circulation. A dry back is less likely to gall than a wet one. Some people find them uncomfortable, and they fit a limited range of horses. Wide animals get sores, or at least pinched by the narrow tree, and the exposed rigging can give the rider a gall as well. Fenders can be added to prevent this.

Advantages of the McClellan include durability and ease of cleaning, since all rigging is exposed. Army-issue rigging can be replaced with nylon, and a sissy pad can be added to the seat if you insist. However, if you find your fanny hurts, it probably means you are

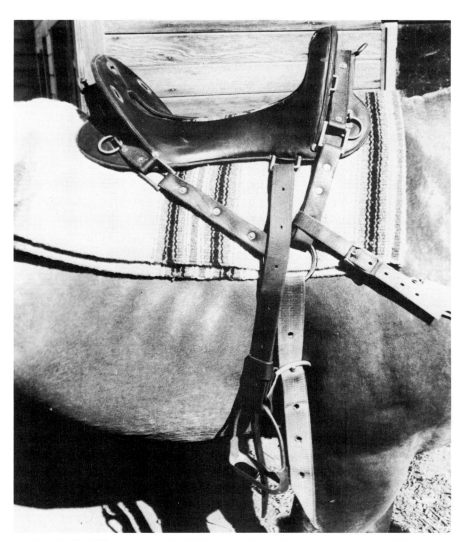

The United States Army McClellan was the original endurance saddle and is still fairly popular. Most specialized endurance saddles borrow design points from the McClellan. This saddle is equipped with nylon rigging for ease of cleaning, and stirrup pads were added to the irons for safety and comfort.

spending too much time on it. You should be posting or in the two-point position much of the time. Both the McClellan and the western saddle allow you to tie a lot of equipment on, using a banana bag. You really don't need to carry a whole lot of gear, so that is a minor concern, except for the convenience of tying a coat on the saddle.

For endurance riding, the rider's weight must be evenly distributed over the horse's back to help prevent fatigue. Weight must be distributed from the center of the saddle out to the edges

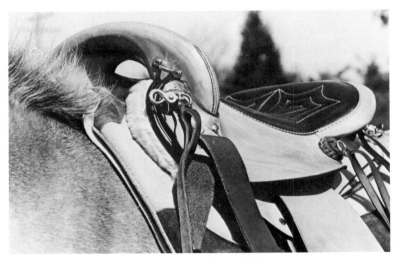

The Sharon Saare endurance saddle was the first mass produced endurance saddle manufactured in this country. Sharon felt there was a need to produce equipment specifically for distance riding after becoming aware of the unsuitability of much equipment being used in the late 1960's and 1970's. "While there may not have been anything inherently wrong with many saddles, they were definitely being used for the wrong purpose. The horses, already working under stress conditions, had to contend with discomfort, and in some cases, injury. Many of the problems related to fit, the differences between endurance type horses and show horses, and the positions the rider wanted to achieve in the saddle. All of these factors were accommodated in the design process."

with only a slight concentration of pressure on the spine.

As the horse tires, his back sags, redistributing pressure over a smaller area to the sides and ends of the saddle. This is where problems begin, particularly if the saddle did not fit well in the first place, or was placed incorrectly on the back.

A September 1978 article in *Equus* magazine discussed saddle fit.* The article stressed the need to place uniform pressure on the weight supporting areas of the back in an area large enough to accommodate that weight without putting it where it doesn't belong. The article explained that the muscle cells and capillaries in the back cannot bear more than one and a half pounds per square inch for lengthy periods of time without damage. They must cope with concussion from the rider that amounts to approximately twice the weight carried—perhaps 300 pounds of pressure from 150 pounds of rider and tack.

A mathematical formula was developed to compute the number of square inches required to equalize the weight over the horse's back:

$$\frac{W \times 2}{1\frac{1}{2}}$$

The total weight of the saddle and rider is multiplied by two, then divided by one and a half, the result equalling the ideal square inches of surface. If the load is 150 pounds, the saddle should have at least 200 inches of weight bearing surface, meaning that a 15-inch saddle should have 14 inches of width in the bars, seven inches on each side. The withers and spine bear no weight.

English saddles have less weight bearing area than stock saddles, and a horse with a very sensitive back may be better off in the larger saddle.

---

* "Before You Saddle Up," *Equus* magazine, copyright © 1978 (Gaithersburg, Maryland 20760).

Placement of the saddle is very important, since too far ahead overloads the forelegs and restricts arm and shoulder motion. Fast gaits place a great load on each front leg, and you don't want to increase that. Too far back will place the saddle over a weak area, tiring the horse quickly. If the bars come over the loin area, the rider can help by riding with weight well forward, but he'll get tired and contribute to eventual back damage.

As the *Equus* article points out, signs of back problems include sinking and flinching from weight, jigging instead of walking or trotting (resulting from bracing the back against pain and not flexing the muscles), tender spots detected by hand pressure, dry spots from excessive pressure which prevents glands from functioning properly, swelling, bald spots or wrinkles. If you note dry spots, resaddle snugly and gradually loosen the saddle over a period of time. The snug cinch simulates the rider's weight, and the pressure prevents excessive swelling and damage. If circulation were restored all at once, weakened capillary walls might give way and worsen the problem. This way they are gradually restored to normal circulation. Wrinkles indicate that the skin is losing its elasticity, and bumps indicate inflammation.

It's a good idea to have more than one type of saddle that fits your horse, as you can alternate during conditioning and change the pressure points.

Fitting a Saddle

These are the steps to determine whether your saddle fits your horse.* Sure, it's a lot of trouble, but it can be worth it.

Place the saddle, without padding, far ahead on the back and slide it back into place. Before fastening the girth, slide your hand under the saddle. If at any point it becomes difficult or impossible to slide your hand between horse and saddle without lifting the

---

* From *Equus* magazine, copyright © 1978 (Equine Health Publications Company, Gaithersburg, Maryland, 20760). reprinted by permission.

saddle with your other hand, that is a point of excessive pressure. Now fasten the girth just tight enough to take the slack out of it without making it tight enough for mounting.

Stand to one side and look down the gullet from the front. You should be able to insert two fingers between the withers and the gullet at the top; there should also be space on either side of the withers. The padding of the bars should rest three-fourths of an inch below the side edge of the withers. Now look up the gullet from the loin; daylight should be visible with one-half inch of clearance between backbone and bars on either side, and no tree contact with the spine.

Standing at the side, grab the cantle and pommel and rock the saddle front to back. If either end rises more than an inch, the tree is too hollow for that back and should be on a horse more swaybacked. If there is no motion at all, the saddle is too flat and the back too hollow; the saddle is "bridging" the gap and placing pressure on the ends only.

Looking under the back of the saddle, make sure the center of the padding on the bars is resting on the back muscles. If the inner edges are the only areas in contact, the saddle is too flat and broad, and there will be pressure injuries along the spine. If the outer edges of the bars make the only contact, the saddle is too narrow, or the horse too fat. Fit will change as condition improves, so check this periodically.

Check the withers and shoulder blades, making sure that the bars don't touch the shoulder blade. If so, the saddle is too far forward. Rotate the shoulder blade by extending the foreleg; the edge of the scapula may rotate beneath the saddle, but not make contact.

Get an assistant to check the fit from the ground while you are mounted. Tighten the girth and repeat all the tests, making sure there is still daylight through the gullet and no rocking. Put a hand between the saddle and shoulder blade as the foreleg is again extended, checking for pinching. There should be no pinching anywhere as you run your hand under the various parts of the saddle. Pinched hand—pinched horse.

Pads and Blankets

The pads used underneath the saddle can help it fit better. You can select from synthetic fuzzy pads, Navajo wool blankets and their copies, and felt or foam pads. Match the pad to the saddle. If you're riding English, don't burden the horse with a large western pad that traps excess heat. English saddles are usually well padded and don't need much extra protection.

A pocket pad works well with the English saddle. It consists of a single thickness of synthetic fiber with pockets that slip over the saddle panels. To make it suitable for endurance, slip a wool blanket, cut to fit, inside it, or use a foam pad. If the saddle tends to set downhill on the horse, making your weight go back too far, tape a large sponge under the cantle area for a boost. This will make you sit more correctly and absorb some of the shock of posting.

Felt pads are good protection since they are dense, but they don't stand up very well to a lot of washing. All the pads you use in this sport will get filthy with sweat and dirt, so they must be washed at least every two weeks, or before a ride. You can use a felt pad inside a pocket fleece pad to keep it clean.

Matthew and Winkie Mackay-Smith use a dense foam pad with a flannel slipcover for endurance work. The flannel is washable and protects the horse from scalding and back irritation. They suggest testing the density of the foam by sitting on a table, using the foam as a cushion. If your seat bones can feel the table, the foam is too thin. This can also be determined by squeezing the foam in between your fingers. Most cheap foam is readily squeezed to paper thickness and provides no protection at all. The pad that the Mackay-Smiths use is quite thin but provides good protection, so thickness is no guarantee of quality.

Slipcovers or external pads can be changed at the half-way stops during a ride so that your horse is always comfortable.

Flow pads are an expensive but effective alternative; they are made especially for endurance work. The outer surface of the pad is wool, and plastic pockets of semi-liquid foam are inserted inside it as padding. The foam is the same as that used in the soles of ski boots to assure full foot contact, and it does the same job for the horse' back. Pressure is uniformly distributed where needed. Unfortunately, the price of a flow pad will buy quite a few less expensive ones.

A wool Navajo blanket over a felt pad, sandwich style, is good protection under a stock or endurance saddle, but can be bulky. It's also expensive, and wool blankets may be a problem to clean. If you use two thick pads, the saddle may be unstable, slipping and causing possible galls. That leaves the acrylic and polyester fuzzy pads, which come in a wide range of prices and are easily washed. They tend to get ratty looking after a while, but it doesn't affect the horse in any way.

Whatever the choice you make for pads and blankets, buy two or more sets so that you can wash them frequently. Dirt is a common cause of back irritation, and one of the easiest to prevent.

Cinches and Girths

Cinches and girths should be made of mohair, or be covered with a girth tube. Mohair softens when wet; nylon cording does not. Mohair is more expensive, and must be washed carefully, as it tends to unravel. It's a good idea to cover mohair cinches and girths to make them last longer. The girths should be wide, and for an English saddle, it's nice to have an anti-chafe girth, shaped to prevent pinching the horse at the elbows. The girths may also have elastic ends to allow the horse plenty of breathing room; you can compensate on plain girths by not doing them up so tightly.

A horse with a good back, coupled with a good breast collar, and perhaps a crupper, will allow you to ride with a fairly slack girth or cinch quite safely. This does require balance and common sense, for you must be alert to impending problems before the situation gets serious. A hard hat might not be a bad idea if you do this much.

Girth tubes and covers are available to match the fuzzy pads, or you can make your own. Wool blanket remnants make good covers that wear well and don't irritate the horse, even if they wrinkle. Wool, a natural fiber, doesn't get as hot as synthetic fibers. Another advantage of wool or other smooth fabric covers is ease of cleaning. When you spend all afternoon picking cockleburs out of a polyester cinch cover, you'll understand.

Plan for two or three sets of tubes and covers for all your tack, including girth, breast collar, and crupper if necessary.

Other Tack Tips

All of your tack should be of good quality leather or nylon. Except for the saddle, nylon is best, since it is machine-washable, unless you have the time and patience to clean each item of leather frequently. Nylon is stronger, but when wet with sweat, it can gall a little, so a cover is a good idea.

Breast collars come in leather, nylon and mohair. There are straight collars, which can be covered with a girth tube for protection, but they may tend to choke. Some have a tie-down strap to keep them in position, which helps. The hunt-type breast collar with neck strap does the best job of keeping an English or endurance saddle in place without cutting off the horse's wind. You can do without a breast collar on some horses, but it's a good item to have, as you don't always realize just how loose your cinch is until you're halfway to the tail.

If your saddle slides forward, a crupper will help keep it in place. If the tail loop causes irritation, a fleece noseband will help prevent chafing and keep it clean. A crupper is an absolute necessity on a mule, and some horses need them, too. Let the horse get acquainted with the crupper during training rides. Taken unaware, he might see it as an excuse to buck.

You may want to consider using padded stirrups, either by covering regular stirrups with foam rubber wrapped with tape or by purchasing special endurance stirrups. The rubber pad used in English irons is usually sufficient, but standing long hours can cause pretty painful feet for some people.

Above all, keep everything in good repair, and keep it clean. While cleaning, look for broken stitches, worn spots, cracks and breaks, and sharp places.

For headgear, use whatever your horse goes best in. A mechanical hackamore or a bosal work best, since they allow the horse to eat and drink freely. If a bit is necessary, choose one without a large mouthpiece, such as a sweetwater instead of a Salinas. The cricket and hood mouthpieces tend to get gunked up if the horse snatches a bite to eat, and they slow drinking quite a bit. A snaffle bit is good if the horse responds to it; a martingale may be necessary to keep the head in position.

The reins can be long split reins, enabling you to tail with them, or a comfortable roping rein of rope or leather. You can add a light nylon rope, about four inches longer than the horse's length from bit to tail, snapping it to the bit on the left side for tailing. This way you can drop the roping rein, jump off and run alongside easily, or drop back and grab his tail. The tailing rope should be knotted so that it doesn't slip through your hand.

When tailing, you can let the horse follow the trail mostly on his own. If he turns right, away from the trail, a tug on the rope will put him back on the track. Going off trail to the left means that you must step to his left side and tug his tail sharply, swinging the hindquarters around a step or two and correcting his position. This takes practice, and a frisky horse at a ride may not be willing to pay attention until he's worn down a little.

A few people find their horses need protective boots, which are allowed under AERC rules. If you use neoprene, keep them washed clean and fasten them securely. They can tear, or be ripped off by thorns. Leather shin boots need a vetwrap underneath to prevent chafing. If bell boots are used, they should be the closed type; they are terrible to put on, but they won't be lost on the trail.

PREVENTIVE MEDICINE

Before conditioning begins, a trip to the veterinarian is in order. Teeth should be floated if necessary, to assure that the horse gets all the nutrients from his feed. The points that develop with excessive wear can cause mouth sores that prevent the horse from eating, and make him difficult to handle.

A worming program should be established. It should be done every six weeks to two months, regardless of fecal check results. As Dr. Matthew Mackay-Smith says, "Don't let the worms stay long enough to lay eggs!" Alternate different classes of wormer to avoid developing a drug-resistant population and assure complete worm control. Do not worm a horse less than two weeks before a ride, as he could become ill from the additional stress.

The horse should have tetanus, flu and sleeping sickness shots, plus any others your vet may recommend. You'll be sharing a lot of water troughs during the months to come; you don't need disease worries. A Coggins test for equine infectious anemia is necessary for interstate travel between some states, and a health certificate may also be needed.

Proper Foot Care

Now that the preventive maintenance is done, let's look at the horse's feet and legs. They are usually the weakest parts of the horse, and you have to take good care of them if you are aiming for a long endurance career. The front tendons seem especially fragile, particularly the right fore. Proper shoeing can help alleviate some of that stress. In a program of defensive shoeing for a horse with park-type action, a two-degree wedge pad is effective in raising the heels. The farrier should also be discouraged from trimming the heels.

The wedge pad, placed with the thickest part under the heel, will shorten the stride and clean up the park action. It cuts some of the horse's efficiency in movement, but it saves a lot of concussion on the forehand and front ligaments. It isn't perfect, though, since the hooves and heels take the pounding that the forelegs originally took. Depending on your horse's style of movement, you may choose either to use wedge pads or to adjust the heel length to compensate.

Rim shoes are the most common in endurance; they are more naturally contoured and allow the horse to balance and turn freely. It's a good idea to have a farrier with endurance experience do the shoeing, as he knows what you are asking for. Of course, you must

Good foot care is extremely important for endurance horses. This horse is in good condition, carrying about the right amount of flesh. It is not a good idea, however, to tie a horse with a chain shank, as he could pull back and hurt himself badly.

caution him *not* to shape the hoof instead of the shoe. Many careless shoers are reluctant to spend an extra minute with the hammer, preferring to clip off any excess horn with the nippers.

Borium extends shoe life, but does not work well for endurance work unless you have a very good farrier. A crude set of borium-plated shoes can cause more problems than they solve, since they don't wear evenly. Uneven spikes form, disrupting the frictional profile and placing stress on the legs.

Bar shoes work in some situations, although they add increased weight to the foot. However, bar shoes do absorb some of the concussion created by wedge pads.

For pads, you can choose from plastic, neoprene or leather. If you plan to modify the horse's way of going, the synthetic wedge pads are your only option. The synthetic pads work better than leather because leather shrinks and swells, depending on ground moisture. This works your shoes loose. Some competitors disdain the use of pads, claiming they add too much weight to the foot and cause the horse to stumble. On the other side of the coin, pads protect your horse in all sorts of trail terrain and can prevent bruises that may take a horse out of competition. This is especially crucial if you are riding fast, unable to avoid rocky patches in the trail.

Before applying the pad, the hoof must be clean, and a coating of ointment or pine tar applied to prevent infection. Oakum is used as a filler under leather pads. It keeps most of the dirt out, but tends to wisp out with wear. Silicone caulking works very well under synthetic pads. It is squirted in with a gun until the void seems to be full. Seal the opening at the heels with tape, such as electrician's tape or duct tape. This keeps the silicone from oozing back out when the horse places weight on the foot. Some will squeeze out anyway; that's life. Stand the horse on a firm surface for an hour or so, to allow the packing to set up thoroughly. You can leave the tape on overnight to be sure.

If you are competing in a ride with sandy stretches, such as beach, you may want to seal the pad opening with tape as a temporary measure. It won't stay on very long, but it will keep some sand from working up under the pad.

One advantage of leather is that you can cut it out after the last ride for that set of shoes to allow the hoof to get some air.

Your horse will need a lot of shoeing, probably every six to eight weeks, depending on shoe wear. Plan your ride schedule, and then your shoeing schedule. Ideally, the shoes should be no more than two weeks old for a tough ride, assuring that the shoes are still secure.

Easyboots. If your horse loses a shoe, or you dislike the idea of metal shoes, Easyboots are another option. They make a handy spare tire, but also give good protection and long wear in many uses, such as on snow and ice, as well as pavement. Hoof injuries can also be treated with the boot.

Neel Glass of Pojoaque, New Mexico, invented the Easyboot. He and his wife Lucille have ridden thousands of miles on their horses, Easyboot Stanley and Easyboot Dandy, using only Easyboots with foam liners. Dandy has never worn a nailed-on shoe.

Easyboots are sized like horseshoes. If you plan to use them over shoes, they should be a larger size than the shoe size to make them easier to get on and off. If used alone, they should match the shoe size.

The Easyboot is applied to a clean hoof, slipping it as far on as possible. Put the hoof down and let the horse finish putting the boot on, just as you stomp into a boot heel. It may be a tough job to get the boot on, but it needs to fit snugly to do the job, and the cable buckle must be as tight as possible.

The inner strap of the boot fits snugly around the quarters below the hairline and the heel bulbs, and its length is adjustable. It may be necessary to trim the back of the boot to prevent chafing. The points of the inner backing plate will scar the wall slightly, but cause no harm. A keeper strap, buckled loosely around the ankle, can be used when fit is doubtful. The Glasses don't recommend using the keeper straps on nervous horses or in fast travel.

A lost Easyboot is easily replaced, but the Glasses suggest checking for perfect fit by pulling the sides outward with a hoof pick, pulling the backing plates away from the wall and seating the hoof completely in the boot. The boot is removed with a hoof pick to unfasten the cable buckle and pull the sides away from the foot; the boot is then pulled off. A short piece of pipe gives more leverage on the buckle if needed.

If you can't get the boot on at all, it's too small. If it flops or pulls off while fastened, it's too big or needs adjustment. For temporary use a piece of foam rubber should be put in the boot. It should reach under the heel strap and upward, to fill the extra space, to provide cushion and to keep dirt out. Silicone caulking

Neel Glass on Easyboot Stanley and Lucille Glass on Easyboot Dandy are still adding up miles to impressive lifetime totals that are in the thousands for both horses. Stanley has over 3,000 miles; Dandy has over 2,500 miles and has never worn anything but Easyboots. The keeper straps are visible around the pasterns in this picture, but the Glasses do not suggest using them when riding fast.

The Easyboot has made it possible for many horses to finish a ride after losing a shoe. It can be used as a spare tire in emergencies, or as permanent footgear. This picture shows the snug fit needed for full effectiveness. In use, the back portion of the boot is trimmed to avoid rubbing the coronary band in any way.

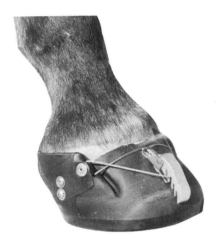

compound and Easyfoam also make good filler. Easyfoam was designed by the Glasses to provide a custom fit to secure the boot. It can be removed after use by soaking the boot in hot water. Lined Easyboots can be left on the foot for up to six weeks if mounted with screws. It is possible that the cable and buckle would pinch the hoof if left too tight for too long. Wedge pads and corrective trimming can be used to correct problems.

When carrying an Easyboot as a spare tire, make sure that it fits the *bare* hoof. Otherwise, it may be too large when the horse loses a shoe and needs the protection. It's also a good idea to check fit on both front and rear hooves, as hind feet tend to be smaller. The boot that fits a forefoot may slip right off the hind, leaving you with a three-footed horse.

One other note—make sure that the boot you carry fits the horse you are riding. If you compete with several horses, it's easy to grab Sunny's boot, only to find that it doesn't fit the mare.

Sheet metal screws with washers, #6 or #8 sizes, are used in mounting the Easyboot for long periods of time. The Glasses say this does no more damage than standard nailing all the way through the hoof, since the screws only penetrate one-quarter of an inch on a normal hoof. A small hole is punched in each side of the boot, even with the top of the E and the T in the lettering on the front. Screws with washers are threaded part way into the holes, and the boot is put on the hoof. The screws are tightened, and that's it.

Easyboots do wear very well in hard use, better than metal shoes.

To keep the hooves healthy and flexible, hoof dressing should be applied daily until the hooves are in good condition, then applied every other day. The dressing should be brushed into the coronary band, the heels and sole. A thin layer over the nails may also do some good, but a coating on the main part of the wall is mostly wasted. The coronary band is the only area where the ointment really does much good. An especially dry hoof can be treated by tying an anklet of wool or fleece around the pastern, where it rubs the coronary band. Soaking that band in ointment every day or so will keep it working on the hoof, constantly working the dressing into it. You can also let the area around the water trough become a little muddy.

Keep in mind that if you're starting with dry, shelly hooves, it can take a year to two years to improve them much, if at all.

WHAT ABOUT FEED?

Now its's time for a look at feed, as that's what makes the horse go. Roughage is the first consideration. Alfalfa hay is very popular with most endurance riders, but the high protein levels seem to have detrimental effects on the horses. It increases the rates of metabolism, causing a slightly higher pulse and respiration. This in itself may be no major problem for ordinary riders, but when it is critical to get down to a certain p/r (pulse/respiration) level in competition, every little bit counts. Protein doesn't break down as cleanly, and doesn't produce as much energy as fat.

Grass hay works very well for endurance horses, and timothy is great if you can get it. Oldtime horsemen never fed alfalfa to horses if timothy was available. Grassy alfalfa may be a good compromise, but you may want to have a protein analysis run so that you know just what you're feeding.

The hay you use should be clean, without a lot of weeds and trash, and bright green, not pale yellow, indicating heavy weathering. There should not be any mold present, and a minimum of dust. Buy your hay from a good farmer who knows what he's doing, or raise your own. Do not buy top bales or bottom bales from hay stacked outdoors. They are weathered and probably slightly spoiled—definitely cow feed.

Endurance horses are fed very little grass since it is essential to control their weight. This means a corral, dry lot or stall to prevent overeating and the resulting "grass belly." Pasture can be allowed on a part-time basis as a reward and a chance to let the horse unwind the week following a ride.

If stabled, an endurance horse must be turned out for several hours a day or exercised religiously on a regular basis. Otherwise he will tear the barn apart or go stir crazy, acquiring one or more nasty vices, such as cribbing or kicking.

Feeding an endurance horse is a controversial subject, and we're still learning about nutrition for these hard-working animals. At this time, there are two major diets for working horses—the high-protein diet, favored by show horse people and quite sufficient for completion of endurance rides, and the high-fat diet, designed to provide maximum energy for serious competitors.

The High-Fat Diet

Dr. Larry Slade of Utah State University studied equine nutrition and developed the basic principles of the high-fat diet. In his paper, "Nutrition for the Equine Athlete," Dr. Slade explains that energy comes from carbohydrates, fats and proteins. Carbohydrates are found in hay and grain starches, and those starches provide blood glucose, a primary energy source for the heart, central nervous system and smooth muscles. Human runners take advantage of this by "carbohydrate loading" prior to a marathon, but a horse cannot do this, as he is suceptible to azoturia (his muscles tying up).

Protein isn't a desirable energy source for the athlete since it doesn't break down as cleanly and burns "hotter." Catabolized carbohydrates have a heat increase of six percent, and fats four percent, but proteins cause a 30 percent increase, placing additional stress on the circulatory system. Excessive protein intake also requires increased water consumption, meaning increased urination and sweating. Slade comments that it is unlikely that horses benefit from extra protein, since the increased regular ration supplies any increased needs for protein when the horse is hard at work.

That leaves body fat as the prime energy source for competing endurance horses. It has been established that more work can be performed under aerobic conditions working on body fat stores than from carbohydrate reserves. Vegetable oil is fed to replace some diet carbohydrates and get more sustained effort from endurance horses by maintaining their blood glucose levels.

Dr. Slade states that several conditions help the horse utilize body fat: pretraining exercise, training diet, work intensity and duration of that work. If the horse trains on a high-fat diet he learns to mobilize his body fats more effectively, since he develops enzyme systems to utilize those fats. When body fat is used for fuel, blood glucose is spared, and the horse can work longer without fatigue.

This radical diet, with 12 percent added fat in the form of vegetable oil, requires careful management on the rider's part. It must be started at least three weeks before a peak effort is planned, and the horse must be regularly exercised. It has been fed to horses for periods up to eight months with no ill effects, and it contributed to a successful 1979 season for the Hollander and Nance families of the Pacific Northwest region. They feel the high-fat diet was a major factor in twelve wins, five second places and seven best condition wins.

However, the high-fat diet isn't for year-round use; a conventional protein-oriented ration is used during the winter and for early training. The horse can then be switched over to the high-fat diet when he begins to get in good condition, indicated when his sweat becomes clear instead of foamy. Twelve pounds of grass hay make up the roughage portion.

The High-Protein Diet

The high-protein diet is suitable for light completion and completion-oriented training programs. If you condition and compete on an irregular basis, the high-protein ration is better suited to your use, and is less expensive. A commercial feed would serve as a basic mix, and you can add the other ingredients as you choose, or you can have feed custom-milled by the ton.

This protein-oriented ration works well when fed as one-third of the total concentrates. Sprouted and whole oats make up the other two thirds.

Whole oats are used because they are high in fiber, palatable to the horse, and easily digested. Rolled oats are more thoroughly digested, but do break down more quickly in storage, losing their nutrients.

Sprouted oats are moist and easily digested, and their vitamin content is greatly increased. They are excellent to feed during an endurance ride, since their extra moisture content helps replenish a dehydrated horse.

The technique of oat sprouting requires seven cheap plastic buckets of the two-gallon size. Punch holes in the bottom of six of them with a hot nail or drill; leave one whole. Put seven nails or pegs in the outside barn wall, near a hose. The bucket without holes is filled half full of oats and then water is added until the bucket is completely full. Soak this overnight; dump the oats into a perforated bucket on peg 2. Wash them off with a hose twice daily.

Fill bucket 1 again, and the next day move bucket 2 to peg 3 to make room for your second batch of wet oats. Continue doing this until all your buckets are full. In three to seven days the oats will sprout, depending on the weather, and you can start feeding them to your horse when the sprouts are almost an inch long. If they do grow excessively before feeding, it doesn't hurt anything.

Depending on the number of horses you are feeding, this process can be adapted to suit your program. Rotating buckets from peg to peg will help assure that you feed the oldest batch of sprouts while they are still fresh. The horses get about two and a half pounds of sprouted oats daily, and the same amount of whole oats. Just start a new bucketful every day so that you don't run out,

Table 2
HIGH-PROTEIN AND HIGH-FAT DIETS

The following are approximate ingredients for one feeding of the high-protein diet and of the high-fat diet as used by Lew Hollander.

HIGH-PROTEIN FEED RATION			HIGH-FAT FEED RATION		
Whole oats	2.5	lbs.	Whole oats	2.5	lbs.
Sprouted oats	2.5	lbs.	Sprouted oats	2.5	lbs.
Corn	1.0	lbs.	Corn	1.75	lbs.
Soybean meal	1.25	lbs.	Fat supplement	1.75	lbs.
Barley	1.0	lbs.	Bran	.75	lbs.
Kelp	.25	lbs.	Yeast	.125	lbs.
Bran	.50	lbs.	Gelatin	.125	lbs.
Calf Manna	.50	lbs.	Kelp	.25	lbs.
Molasses	.50	lbs.			
Yeast	.125	lbs.			
Gelatin	.125	lbs.			

and don't forget to rinse each bucket twice a day.

In the high-fat diet, protein levels are held to about seven percent overall, while the fat levels range from 10 to 12 percent. To achieve this, corn and bran quantities are increased. Oil may be added, as Dr. Slade suggests. Quantities range from four cups daily to four pounds, fed by Dr. R. A. Beecher. Both Slade and Beecher say they have had no palatability problems or diarrhea associated with this diet.

As used by the Hollanders and Nances, *corn* is the basis for this high-fat diet since it is the "hottest" of the cereal grains, with more calories. Bran helps to keep the horse's digestive system in working order and aids in supplying more energy. Bran and kelp are both high in protein, and their benefits outweigh their drawbacks. Kelp supplies trace minerals—an important addition to a horse's diet, although some authorities caution that iodine can accumulate to toxic levels. Yeast supplies B vitamins in large quantities.

The gelatin is added to provide the necessary amino acids for good hoof growth. Research has not proven any conclusive connection, but it seems to help. Endurance horse nutrition is unique, since the horses use up tremendous quantities of nutritients. A shortage that isn't noticeable in the arena horse could have disastrous effects on an endurance horse.

In addition, various supplements are added to the high-fat diet. Selenium, in the form of SE90, is added at the rate of eight milligrams a week. Requirements differ in various parts of the country, so consult a veterinarian or nutritionist for requirements in your area. Selenium was recently legalized as a commercial salt additive, so check everything you feed to make sure that your horse doesn't get an overdose. Selenium is cumulative, and in large quantities it becomes toxic, causing hair loss and abnormal hoof growth.

Another source of selenium is E-Se, an injected supplement available from your veterinarian. Selenium and Vitamin E seem to work together in some undetermined way, and Dr. Slade believes that endurance horses need 4,000 to 4,500 IU (International Units) of Vitamin E for optimum performance. It is especially essential to supply extra Vitamin E when unsaturated oils are added to the feed, since these oils accelerate the use of E and increase the need. There is no toxicity problem with excess Vitamin E.

Giving frequent shots can be a nuisance, but it is a certain way to know just what your horse is getting. Follow the vet's recommendations as to quantity, as the amount your horse needs will vary according to the amount of selenium in your soil and forage.

Selenium and Vitamin E do seem to prevent tying up (azoturia), and thereby help protect your horse. Dr. Beecher said in a speech at the 1980 AERC convention that baking soda can also help horses with a history of tying up. He suggests feeding a tablespoon daily, thinking that it may work like an equine Rolaid to settle the horse's stomach and dissipate lactic acid.

Beecher feeds feed-grade sodium bicarbonate (baking soda) free choice, and finds that his horses consume it freely as needed. He finds it especially good following a ride. Beecher also pointed out that sodium bicarbonate is used in dairy cattle feed to improve their fat utilization, and suggests that it may work the same way with horses. This is not yet proven.

A good vitamin supplement with A, D and E is used in the Hollander-Nance high-fat ration as a preventive measure. Most of the time the horse's vitamin needs are supplied in his normal ration, but when under stress, his need for them increases dramatically. A free-choice mineral mix is always available to the horse. Di-calcium phosphate is added to balance the calcium-phosphorus ratio at approximately one to one. The molasses holds everything together and enhances the taste to the horse.

Whatever you feed your horse, feed it regularly and frequently. Large quantities of concentrates should be divided into at least two feedings, preferably three or even four.

The Role of Electrolytes

The final subject in this chapter is electrolyte supplementation, an essential subject. There are riders who claim to use no added electrolytes, but they may not be doing as well as they possibly could. It is possible that some horses do better on their own, but it is known that the active horse suffers a significant depletion of water and salt, as well as magnesium, calcium and potassium. Those minerals are used in muscular activity and lost in the sweat, as evidenced by the white crusting often seen on horses after a hard workout.

Electrolytes are available from your veterinarian in bolus and powder forms, or you can mix your own. "Lew's Mix" is described in Appendix B. It is much cheaper than commercial supplements, but contains nearly the same ingredients—sodium chloride, potassium chloride and magnesium sulphate. That translates to table salt, Lite Salt and epsom salts, and the formula has proven effective at a cost of two cents a dose, compared to up to 50 cents a dose for some brands.

You shouldn't oversupplement electrolytes, as this isn't a case of "if a little is good, more is better." An excess can cause a chemical imbalance in the horse, leaving him worse off than before.

Whenever the horse sweats heavily, he could use a small amount in his feed. Amounts vary according to formulation, and you should follow the manufacturer's suggestions. When using "Lew's Mix," approximately two teaspoonfuls are sufficient.

Electrolytes are added to the feed during the three days prior to a ride, and during and after the ride they are given orally with a clean wormer syringe. This procedure is detailed in Chapter 5.

Don't hesitate to adjust the ration if the horse isn't doing well on it. If he's too thin, he needs more grain or a higher fat level. If he's overweight, cut the feed or increase the work.

4: Conditioning the Endurance Horse

WHEN YOU BEGIN the work of conditioning your endurance horse, keep in mind that you have an entire horse to develop and strengthen through sensible work. The heart can be conditioned in six months, and the muscles in approximately a year, but tendons and ligaments take up to two years for full improvement, and joints require three years. This means that conditioning must be carried out over a period of years for the best effect. Bones take the longest time, from two to four years.

Most of the essential development for endurance can take place in a year, but overstressing the legs before they are ready can eliminate the endurance prospect from further testing. Most endurance horses don't come into their prime until they've traveled a good thousand miles, and then only if they're ridden sensibly and are well cared for.

Physical modification of the horse begins early in life, almost at birth for the range-raised colt, and at the age of two for most horses. The colt started for flat racing at two will have superb cardiovascular development, but his legs may not be strong enough to sustain endurance effort for long.

This is why so many horses appear as superstars for one year— then vanish into limbo, while others go trucking along for 10 years or more. Another reason for a long, slow training program is that many problems will disappear as the horse matures. Some horses are able to dash right out and start winning, but the odds are against a long, successful career for them.

Conditioning will improve the heart's ability to circulate blood, and increase the oxygen capacity of the blood. Muscle strength and stamina increase, and the waste elimination system improves in order to handle the toxins produced by exercise. The horse's body becomes more efficient at dispersing heat after hard work, and his lungs do a more effective job of taking in air and exhausting heat. The nervous system learns to handle the stress. Don't underestimate a horse's mind because it can be just as hard to deal with a horse that thinks he's tired as one that's truly weary.

Conditioning is _not_ going out and riding the stuffing out of the horse day after day. If the horse is coming back exhausted from his workouts, he's going to learn to hate you and the entire idea of riding. There should always be a little bit left in the gas tank to come home on, building the horse's confidence in doing the job. If someone told you that you were going to run marathons, starting right now, and sent you out on the course with a whip, you would soon be discouraged and angry. But if they asked you to run the mile first, and gradually work up in distance, you might even enjoy this.

The entire object of conditioning is to stress the systems enough to make them work harder than normal without causing damage. Every rider has a different way to condition, and the distance typically used is often determined by the handiest loop trail. Every horse differs, too, and the training program must be adjusted to compensate.

The original idea of proper conditioning was miles and miles of slow work. That is only the start. The Hollanders were at a runner's seminar one year when the speaker said, "If you train long and slow, you'll be a long, slow runner, and if you train short and fast, hopefully you'll be a faster long runner." That means interval training, and it applies to horses as well as people. The principle of interval training is to alternate work with rest sessions, allowing more total work in a workout. Short, repeated stresses in interval work can be alternated with distance workouts to build speed, increase stamina, increase the potential heart rate and lower the working pulse for ordinary work.

Checking your horse's pulse will give you an idea of the stress he is currently feeling, and recovery after a few minutes will indicate his condition. The inside of the jawbone, where an artery crosses, is an easy place for checking the pulse with your fingers.

The pulse may also be taken in the girth area, just behind the elbow. A stethoscope works best here, but your fingers can also do the job. The stirrup should be run up the leather, as shown here, or put over the horn to keep it out of the way.

UNDERSTANDING THE VITAL SIGNS

Before you begin conditioning, learn to take pulse and respiration counts. You can take a pulse by hand, or use a stethoscope. The stethoscope does allow you to listen to the pulse and detect abnormalities, and it makes it easier to pick up gut noises from the digestive process, letting you know how tired your horse is. Respiration is taken by observation. You need a watch with a second hand for both.

Locate the pulse on your horse. It may be easiest the first time to do it after a brisk workout, when the pulse is faster and stronger. The girth area, just behind the horse's elbow on the left side, is a good spot for a stethoscope check. The inside of the left jawbone, where an artery crosses, is a good place when you are using your fingers, and the pulse can also be detected in the pastern, just above the bulbs of the heel. The jaw is the easiest place on a saddled horse, and you can keep the head still while you locate the pulse. If he eats while you're taking the pulse elsewhere, it distracts you, and the racket makes it impossible to hear through the stethoscope.

After detecting the pulse, count for 15 seconds and multiply by four for the rate per minute. Listening through a stethoscope, the pulse sounds like *lub dup, lub dup.* Count only the strongest beat of the pair, or the *lubs.* When taking the pulse by feel, you'll only detect a single beat, the one that contracts the heart. The second beat is the sound of the aorta rebounding after the heart valves close. Occasionally a p/r person at a ride will count both beats and get an astronomical result from "double pulsing." When in doubt, do it over.

The average resting pulse ranges from 32 to 44 beats a minute, with stallions often ranging from 28 to 36 beats per minute. At work, the pulse may go as high as 200 beats a minute in extreme stress, but you should train at approximately 100 beats a minute. When it is 60 beats or less per minute, the horse is recovered and ready for additional work.

Respiration may be taken by holding your hand near the left flank, close but not touching. As the horse breathes, the distance between your hand and the flank decreases, and that's what you count. Count for 15 seconds and multiply by four for the rate per minute. You can also take respiration counts by holding your hand in front of the nostrils, but this is inaccurate, particularly when strangers do it. The horse will sniff at their hand, disrupting the breathing pattern. Respiration can be very difficult to observe in a rested horse since the flank motion is so slight.

Typical respiration levels are from 8 to 16 per minute, usually in a 3 to 1 ratio with pulse. Normally it is less than the pulse count; when respiration counts are higher than pulse, it is known as an inversion, and signifies that the horse is overheated and panting. It is not a major concern unless the body temperature is excessively high.

Temperature, taken with a rectal thermometer, has a normal range of 99° to 101.5° Fahrenheit. For a horse at rest, fever is indicated if the reading is more than two degrees above normal, but a horse at work would be okay as long as the temperature was not much over 103.5°. He will probably pant to cool himself until the body temperature is lowered to 101° or 102°.

Log the results of your vital-signs checks until you learn the normal pulse and respiration counts for your horse at rest. In training you will be primarily concerned with pulse counts since they are simple and fast to take while providing an accurate indication of how your training is progressing. The key is not how high it gets, but how fast it goes back down to below 60 beats a minute.

Most horses begin to drop within five minutes of ceasing exercise; a fit horse begins to recover within five seconds. At rides you will often have to meet a 64-pulse requirement, so train to that or less to assure a good margin. Requiring a lower recovery level in training also helps assure that the horse isn't overworked when he isn't ready. When he can recover from 90 to 60 beats a minute in just a few minutes, your conditioning program is taking effect.

Respiration may be checked by holding your hand just in front of the nostrils to feel each breath. This can be inaccurate, as the horse may sniff at your hand or be otherwise disturbed by a stranger's hand.

You can also check respiration by holding your hand near, but not touching, the flank. As the flank moves with each breath, the distance between your hand and the horse decreases, allowing you to make a fairly accurate count. If the horse is breathing so slowly you can't count it, don't worry. He's fine.

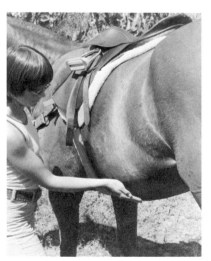

A green horse can be conditioned to *complete* a slow endurance ride in six months or so, but it takes much longer to build the extra conditioning that makes a winner.

When your conditioning program begins, the horse should be trim, not overweight. The horse just off the track will be in great shape to begin work, but the marshmallow needs months of slow, slow work to peel off the pounds before starting serious work. The ribs should be visible when the horse is in motion, but not obvious when he is at rest.

An underweight horse is either overconditioned or underfed, and in either case, has no reserves left. This happens when riders get so enthusiastic that they ride 30 miles a day for weeks at a time. When the horse comes to a ride, he's already worn out. A horse can also get underweight when the rider tries to starve blubber off instead of feeding small quantities and riding the fat off. Raw-boned horses are not only in poor condition, but project a poor image for the sport. Don't get your horse so thin that you have to hide him behind the barn. If his hair is frizzy and dry, and he lacks energy and impulsion, he is overconditioned. It will be a

This hot walker has sawdust placed in the "circle" for good footing, and is lined with tires to prevent short-cutting by the horses. A walker should be reversible, as it can strain the horses when only used in one direction. It also can teach bad habits, like cocking the head.

long time before he's back to peak condition.

In early spring the horse will still be pretty hairy, and a trace clip is a good idea if you can stable the horse at night, or even a body clip. In a *trace* clip, hair is trimmed on the lower neck and body, leaving a complete coat on the back and legs for protection against the elements. It looks like the dickens but makes it much easier to cool the horse, preventing possible pneumonia and saving time. Clipping the long, shaggy hair on the legs makes them easier to clean, but don't trim the hair too short, as it can dig in and irritate the leg. This could contribute to a case of scratches, a kind of rash that is further irritated by sweat, dirt and dust. Some hair should be left on the legs for protection against brush and thorns.

LEGGING UP

Dr. Matthew Mackay-Smith comments that you should plan training sessions to stress the weakest system in the horse without overdoing it. Repeated work at levels just below maximum capability with rest breaks will improve the horse, while extreme stress for long periods of time does no good. During initial "legging up" the horse will be asked to maintain a moderate rate of stress for ten miles or so, but you would not ask him to go out and run the distance. Instead, you ask him to trot as much of the distance as he can, gradually increasing the trotting until there are few or no breaks in gait.

Legging up can be a brief process for the ranch or race horse with a work history, and a tedious one for the backyard pet or halter horse. A horse being trained hard in dressage and jumping will be ready to go out and trot 10 miles almost at once.

A walker can be used for some of the initial training if you do not plan schooling your horse in other events. The Hollanders condition their horses early in the season with daily sessions on the walker, at 10 miles an hour for an hour in both directions.

Veteran horses need little preliminary legging up before starting interval work.

The hazards of using a hot walker include sourness and stress from the constant circling. If you use one, it should have the longest arms available, and variable speeds and direction. If a horse begins to balk, you'll have to get after him to make him work. A walker does make it easy to give the horse a steady workout without the stress of carrying weight.

If you choose not to use a walker, an hour's hard training or ten miles of riding are a good substitute.

In the Hollander training program, a five-year-old is broken and learns his manners, but waits to begin distance work at age six. At that time he gets ten miles daily at a trot for three to six months, then starts interval training. He is taken through three or four slow endurance rides at a walk by a light rider. The conditioning process continues at age seven, more speed is asked, and at age eight, he is asked for all he has. Obviously you must start with a likely prospect to make it worth all the time you put in.

THE TRAINING HILL

A horse that has been conditioned before will get into shape quickly, and he can alternate days on the walker with days of interval work on the training hill. Six weeks of this puts a horse in pretty fair shape, but it's a good idea to take it easy for the first ride or two.

The Hollander training program has almost eliminated the weekly long ride that most riders use, and their horses seldom go more than 15 to 20 miles a day. The training hill is about seven miles from where they park the trailer, so the horses warm up at a brisk trot before the interval work begins.

It's a good idea to condition more than one horse at a time so that you have a spare. You can pony the spare on training rides and swap every 10 miles, or tie him up until you're ready to give him his interval training.

The hill has a slope of 15 degrees, and the horses are asked to gallop up it, a distance of half a mile over rocky ground. The stress is obvious at first when they reach the top; where the riders dismount and lead the horses back to the bottom at a trot, saving the forelegs. A pulse count is taken at the bottom, and when the horses have recuperated to 64 beats a minute or so, it's time for another dash up the hill. When the horses can manage four sprints in a day, they are in condition for a ride.

Using the same course over and over for training allows you to compare recoveries and see visible improvement. During races the horses maintain high performance levels for hours even though the training time was comparatively short. Instead of increasing miles and the risk of injury, sprints are added to peak the horse out. The program is the same whether conditioning for a 50- or 100-mile ride, since the horse is either in shape, or he isn't.

As condition improves, the horse's sweat will no longer be lathery, but thin and clear. The first sweat of the day might be frothy from dirt, but will clear as the day goes on. Lather between the hindlegs indicates the horse is using his hindquarters and working instead of loafing. If weather permits, bathe the horse after a workout, perhaps putting a dash of liniment in the water to make him feel better. After he's washed, he'll roll, but that will be "clean" surface dirt, not the irritating sweat and crud that can cause skin problems.

The horse needs to be worked six days a week in preliminary conditioning, with one day of turn-out or longeing for exercise. For longeing the horse should be on a rope at least 25 feet in length, or even longer to allow a generous circle. A minimum of ten minutes each direction at an energetic trot and canter will show results. This gives you a chance to teach verbal commands, later useful in tailing, and don't hesitate to set the horse down hard if he ignores you.

Before you start teaching him to tail, make sure he hasn't any ticklish spots or a tendency to kick. You should be able to rub him anywhere under the belly and between the legs. Sometimes strange accidents happen and you have to crawl out from beneath the horse, or even through him on a very narrow trail. This isn't a good idea, but sometimes there is no choice.

THE CONDITIONING SCHEDULE

If the weather permits, training usually starts in January or February for April rides. Conventional training schedules suggest starting out with up to seven miles several days a week for the first month. In the winter that's about all you can do. The horse is ridden up to 9 miles a day in the second month and 15 miles in the third month. In the final month of conditioning the horse may be asked to do 25, 15 and 9 miles in three outings a week with longeing on the days off. By the time the season begins, the basic conditioning is complete and the horse is gradually peaked out.

Miss Fit, the 1974 national champion, ridden by Elwin Wines, was conditioned by his kids during the winter. The Wines family lived three miles from the highway, and the kids rode the horses downhill at a brisk trot to catch the school bus. At night they galloped home, and this went on all winter, six miles daily, five days a week. When spring came Elwin had the kids take a longer route home with a two and a half mile climb, and the horses galloped it easily the first time. An occasional ten-mile gallop was thrown in to improve Miss Fit's recoveries, and that was all it took.

Endurance horses learn to hold a brisk trot on a loose rein. When they want to stop, push them a little farther and let it be *your* idea to walk. Most riders allow the horse to select his own speed of trot, letting him learn to rate himself. The miles may seem long to you, but the horse cannot count or read, so he doesn't comprehend how far it is from here to there. He only knows that he has to get there before he can go home. Signs of tiring include forging and interfering, and indicate that you should give him a breather.

A few riders start their horses barefoot to teach them to look out for the rocks, and to encourage a lighter forehand when descending hills. This has its merits, but it doesn't please the shoer when he has to tack shoes onto cracked and broken walls.

MORE ABOUT HILLS

Hills are the very best places to condition, since just walking up is good exercise. You get more conditioning with less time put in. Hill work is absolutely essential if you plan to enter mountain rides, and the horse needs to learn to balance himself going downhill.

There are two schools of thought on this. One insists that the horse has a limited number of fast downhill miles in him, and that they should be saved for the rides. The other faction believes the horse needs to learn to take care of himself, starting with slow trotting on slight slopes. This is a reasonable view, but it requires good sense and patience. It can take up to two years to teach a horse to go downhill well.

To go downhill well the horse must be slightly collected, placing most of his weight on the hindquarters. Starting with a slow trot for short distances, gradually ask the horse to go a little farther and a little faster. Eventually he will be able to glide downhill as if he were on wheels, but if you overdo it too soon, the front legs can suffer. A green horse may lose control of himself and go rocketing down the hill, just like you if you run too fast downhill.

Cliff Lewis, an experienced rider with thousands of miles, conducted an experiment to see whether it was easier on the horses to be led downhill at a trot, or ridden downhill. He had a good runner lead a horse down a long hill while he rode another, and found at the bottom that recovery times were nearly identical. The ridden horse did slightly better at times.

This requires excellent horsemanship and a balanced seat so that you don't interfere with the horse. This will be discussed in detail later in the chapter.

If you haven't got hills to condition on, you can get some of the same effects by riding up and down the sides of a sand pit (barrow pit) for an hour. Walking up and down a creek is also good exercise since the horse must deal with the resistance of the water and the muddy stream bed. If the bottom is rocky and slick, find someplace else to ride. If you're going to rides that are on soft

After the initial legging-up period, galloping on good ground and over medium hills will bring the horse's condition to its peak. Hanne Hollander demonstrates a good riding position that helps Law Thunder as much as possible.

ground, the horse must learn to deal with the extra work.

On the other hand, if you've only got soft ground to train on, slow work on pavement can simulate working on rocks. This must be started slowly, as splints and other leg problems develop when a horse is asked for too much too soon. Joggers have the same problems.

Skidding a log or railroad tie is a good way to exercise the hill-climbing muscles, and is a useful skill. Harrow the pasture while you train. Treadmills haven't been around long enough to really determine how well they work for endurance horses, but they are reputedly excellent for teaching the horse to move out and use the hindquarters efficiently. However, the expense prices many endurance people out of the market.

BUILDING UP THE STRESS

The Mackay-Smiths comment that the horse shouldn't be asked for a top effort in the first three months of training, saying that 7 to 11 miles an hour over easy terrain is enough. If the country is absolutely flat the horse will have to go at least ten miles an hour to improve. As he gets accustomed to that the distance is increased, up to a maximum of 40 miles. Needless to say, you do not ride 40 miles every day, as that is too much.

Approximately three months prior to the first rides the horses are asked to go faster over a distance of 10 to 20 miles. This develops maximum aerobic capacity as the horse learns to use oxygen efficiently, enabling him to go faster. The maximum aerobic rate for most horses is about 120 to 130 beats per minute, and an ideal training level seems to be on the strong side of 100 beats a minute. Above 130 to 150 beats per minute the body goes into anaerobic function since the demands can no longer be met by the oxygen intake. An oxygen debt is incurred, and the horse will wear out more quickly.

The horse is being stressed when either his pulse or his respiration are over 100, or the combined total is over 180. When he can recover to near-normal levels in 5 to 10 minutes or less, he's coming along.

The problem you now face is keeping the horse at near-peak condition without overworking him. Maintenance of the horse's condition is done with a couple days of interval work each week, or a two-mile gallop twice a week. Extensive galloping should be done on a race track, dirt road or fallow field to protect the feet and legs. It doesn't take nearly as much work to keep the horse in shape as it did to get him there. On days off, the horse should be longed and his feed cut accordingly, especially if he gets no exercise at all.

A regular schedule must be established after you decide which rides to attend during the season. The ideal would probably be one ride monthly, allowing the horse to fully recover between rides. This limited schedule is necessary only if you are racing instead of just riding for completion; the average horse can handle two rides a month with ease as long as he is ridden sensibly.

CHOOSING THE RIGHT RIDE

In deciding the length of rides that you want to enter, bear in mind that 25-milers are nothing but demolition derbies that encourage rough riding. Since the distance is short, there is no let up throughout the route, and the horses suffer as a result. A 25-mile ride is meaningless on a career record; it is not counted on either horse or rider mileage totals. With the expense of travel and entries, 25-mile rides are a waste of money. Another problem with 25-mile rides is that the horse learns he can quit when he begins to tire a little. And a 50-mile ride isn't that much harder.

In contrast, a relaxed 100-mile ride over easy terrain builds the horse up instead of tearing him down. The longer rides are much easier on the horse since the pace is slower. A 50-mile ride ridden to win can turn into four 12-mile sprints. This is mainly true on the flat rides; on mountain rides, even the hotshot riders back off to a reasonable speed. Almost any horse capable of completing a 50-miler in good time, say six hours or less, is capable of a conservative 100-miler.

Pre- and Post-Ride Routine

Now let's look at the week before a ride scheduled for Saturday. This is Monday, you will work the horse tomorrow, Tuesday, and give him a good run on Wednesday, using the training hill or a track. It's not the time to put a lot of miles on him, since he should be in condition by now. The horse remains on full feed through Wednesday, then gets cut to about half on Thursday and Friday to correspond with the reduction in exercise. Longeing or time on the walker will be enough work those two days, letting the horse rest.

If the ride is a 100-miler, the horse gets his full ration on Friday night, since he needs all the calories he can get. For a 50-miler, he remains on half rations, since he'll run better empty on a short ride.

The week following the ride should be spent in the pasture if possible, allowing the horse to relax. If he had problems during the ride, or ran especially hard, he might need two or three weeks before another start. It never hurts to give the horse a little extra time off with moderate training. It's ideal to have two horses to campaign, since you can ride more frequently that way. It is possible to take the same horse to a ride only a week later, but only if you're prepared to do a lot of walking. Some horses can handle the stress after they've gotten a lot of experience, but the green horse would be better off with fewer, longer rides.

One of the problens in maintaining a competitive horse at his peak is boredom. Trail riding exclusively is a good way to bore him to death. A horse show or play day makes a good change, or you can teach the horse something new, like jumping.

Jumping is a useful skill for the trail horse since it teaches him to stride into obstacles smoothly and quietly, using his muscles and momentum efficiently. He'll be able to step smoothly through cluttered trails, knowing where his feet will land, and skim over logs and ditches easily. He won't waste effort soaring six feet into the air to cross a small obstacle. Besides, it's fun!

During your training and competing, ask yourself if your horse really likes this, or if he's just cooperating with a whim of yours. If he has no natural aptitude and seems to hate the long rides, perhaps this isn't his niche. But if he adores the competition and the challenges, you could have a tough horse to beat. Don't hesitate to adapt your training program or do something different for a while to break up the monotony. You're dealing with a live animal who has his own thoughts and opinions on the sport, and he's bigger than you are.

At the season's end, let the horse down gradually with decreasing exercise. Substitute turning out for long rides, and gradually cut the feed to the working level for the winter. If the horse will be turned out all winter, only a small amount of grain is necessary. Bad weather will increase the number of calories he needs, but in general, good hay and a small snack is plenty. Shoes are pulled to allow the hooves to expand and get back to normal.

In the course of a layoff, some conditioning will be retained, and that residual conditioning will speed up the process of preparing for next year's rides.

ENDURANCE EQUITATION

Now that the horse's conditioning has been discussed, let's look at endurance equitation. You're training an athlete and you must be able to ride him. An uncertain or weak rider can ruin a willing horse, and poor equitation can hurt you both. If your balance is poor and you are more concerned with your aches and pains than the horse, you aren't helping him at all.

You must ride a good balanced seat, learned with a few riding lessons and lots of miles. It puts you over the center of gravity where the horse can carry weight most easily, in the same position used by hunt-seat riders on the flat and dressage riders. Don't think that only the English riders can do it—look at the pictures of the Old West by Charles Russell. His cowhands sat with long stirrups, feet slightly ahead, and a relaxed body. They rode for a living, and had to be comfortable. You're not going to survive well at this unless you are at home on a horse—any stiffness in your body will cause a great deal of discomfort during and after the rides.

Too many careless riders sit on their pockets and poke their feet way ahead in the "chair" seat. By sitting this way, the horse is being told to slow down and shorten his strides. His kidneys hurt, his back is hollowed out, and he can't figure out why in heck you are laying into him with the whip. This sounds amusing, but it's the truth. There are riders who lean backward and hold onto the cantle while whipping the horse over and under to make him go.

The correct position shared by all good horsemen who ride a balanced seat starts with correct stirrup length. The stirrups should be set at arm's length, or ankle bone length, allowing your leg

This is the correct position for distance riding, forward over the horse's center of gravity and balanced lightly in the stirrups. However, don't wear a heavy jacket unless the weather is very cold, as you will warm up a great deal while riding and get quite uncomfortable.

to be bent comfortably with the foot bent back underneath. It seems awkward, but is quite comfortable, and makes it easy to stand in the two-point position for long distances. Do not make the mistake of setting the stirrups short enough to force your knees into the knee rolls of a jumping saddle. You are not going over high fences, and your legs will be killing you in just a few miles if you don't put those irons down where they belong.

The traditional straight line should go down your back and through your heels. You won't be sitting straight every minute, but you should keep the basic position in mind. Don't slouch off sideways, and don't hook a leg over the saddle horn. If you can't sit right, get off and walk.

You will be forward whenever you ride at speed, and your stirrups, if set correctly, will allow you to just clear the saddle seat when you stand in them. This is the "up" position when you post, and the two-point position used at the canter and gallop. The trot is never sat in competition, as that tires the horse's back more quickly and increases the chance of soreness. Diagonals at the trot and leads at the canter are alternated to use different sets of muscles.

Much of the time you'll balance freely in the saddle, grasping a bit of mane or the saddle to stay upright. You shouldn't clear the saddle by more than an inch, as you could topple back into the saddle and really disturb the horse. It's also much harder on your own back.

On hills, you ride in the two-point position, staying well forward. This allows the hindlegs to drive well under the horse and push him up the hill. Downhill, you sit as you would for the sitting trot on the flat, not leaning backward, but sitting upright and keeping your feet underneath you. In an English saddle, pushing your knees into the knee rolls will help you stay in position as you trot or walk down the hill.

If you're sitting correctly, you may feel awkward and rigid at first until you learn to relax. As you gain confidence your riding

A fresh horse on a high-energy diet can be a real handful for the first few miles, especially if he learns to take advantage of you. Good equitation will save your neck on these occasions, as shown here by this rider's position. His weight is forward so that the mare doesn't topple backward; his legs are at the girth, driving her forward and onto her feet.

will improve, allowing you to go faster through rough ground without constantly checking the horse. Controlling the horse will also be much easier, especially during the first few miles of a ride.

Of course there won't be anyone handing out ribbons for good horsemanship at the rides, but good riding gets good placings. A good rider can take a mediocre horse to the top; a poor one can utterly destroy the chances of a champion.

Good riding isn't easy; your back will ache and you'll be exhausted after a ride. Your legs will be pretty shaky and your feet might even be sore from standing in the stirrups. But if it saves the tiniest bit of energy for your horse, it's worth it. Whose back would you rather see aching? Yours, or the horse's? The answer should be yours if you want to be a serious competitor. The horse is doing a lot of work for you; you should help him along the way.

5: Go Slow and Get There Quicker

WHEN YOU'RE READY for your first endurance ride, don't choose the roughest one you can find, unless you have an experienced horse. A 50-miler is the best way to break in; 25 miles is a waste of time, and a good way to hurt the horse. It's just too tempting to race the short distance, and consequently ride the horse right into the ground. Keep in mind that your first endurance ride is going to be unlike any experience you ever had in your whole life, regardless of the amount of training you've done.

A few rides ask that you pre-enter, so they can arrange for awards and dinner, if any. At some rides, you may have the option of completion certificates for a lesser fee instead of the expensive award. Family rates are also offered by a few rides, with discounts on more than one or two entries. This can really help if you have three or four people riding, as entry fees can range from $35 to $70 or more.

THE RIDE REGIMEN

Plan to arrive at the ride the day before, preferably in daylight. There'll be people pulling in all night, though, so don't worry if you just can't make it by the deadline. Late horses are vetted in by flashlight, or early the next morning, so don't worry that they won't let you enter. All but a few rides are glad to take your money, no matter when you arrive. If you know you'll be late, it might be a good idea to pre-enter, or call ahead to let the secretary know about you.

Be sure to protect your horse's legs with shipping boots or

bandages, plus bell boots if they scramble. It is a time-consuming chore, but it is cheap insurance. When some idiot stops right in front of you and you have to stack all the horses on their noses to stop, you'll be glad those legs are protected.

Accidents on the road aren't unheard of. If you haven't much experience in pulling a trailer, get someone to show you the tricks. For instance, don't speed up coming out of a curve until the trailer is straight, or the horses will "crack the whip." A few corners and they'll begin tearing the trailer apart in their efforts to stand up.

The horses should have hay while they travel, and most people unload every 300 to 400 miles to let the horses relax. Some horsemen haul tremendous distances without stopping, but in the typical horse trailer, your horse needs that break. He can't stretch out to urinate comfortably, and he may refuse to drink while inside. Of course, if the horse is a holy terror to load, you may not want to risk unloading him. If he has a problem, train him at home before going to rides. A trailer-fighter runs a high risk of injury before he ever gets to the ride, and with the current price of gas, why drive 500 miles, only to withdraw?

Finding the ride site isn't too difficult. Signs are usually up, and course ribbons are often used to indicate that you're going in the right direction. The information sheet usually has a map or detailed directions on it.

Setting up Camp

The first thing you do when you arrive is park on a good level spot. Get the horses out and unwrapped. Let them walk around and stretch, and have a good drink. It's a good idea to park as close as possible to the water supply, unless you enjoy carrying 80 pounds of water three times a day for half a mile.

A portable corral is very handy on endurance rides, as it lets your horses relax and move around as they wish. They come in *pvc* pipe, steel, and homemade variations. Some people set up a hot fence with a battery-powered charger.

If you haven't a corral, the horses will spend their time tied to the trailer, with their ropes just long enough to reach the ground comfortably. You'll see ropes twice as long as needed, but a horse can get rope-burned easily, putting you out of the ride. If you want him to graze, hold the rope, or put him on a picket line. However, don't leave him picketed overnight because he can easily get entangled.

The hay goes in a hay net, tied high enough to stay well clear of the forefeet. A horse that paws while eating can get all tangled up in a sagging net. There are dozens of ways for a horse to get hurt, and he'll do his darndest to find every one.

You can purchase or make brackets that mount on the trailer to hold your grain and water buckets, or you can just set them on the ground to be spilled. You'll probably find the brackets pay for themselves with the feed they save.

Of course you'll have a good halter and lead rope, and perhaps two lead ropes on a horse that fights being tied. A loose endurance horse can run 10 miles before he stops, so don't give him that opportunity.

Registration

After the horses are comfortable, go enter the ride. They will have plenty of time to eat while you wait in line. If your horse is registered, carry copies of his papers for verification. You will not be eligible for breed awards without them. Enter him under his registered name so that there won't be any confusion later about what horse you rode. You'll receive a pinney, or numbered pouch, to identify you during the ride and hold your rider card, which records times and vital signs throughout the ride.

After you have registered, you go get the horse for his preliminary vet check. Make sure that you can control him. If you think he might pull away from you, or refuse to stand, use a stud chain over his nose to get his attention. It makes a poor impression when your horse kicks the vet, and an unruly horse can be disqualified.

While you wait for the vet, a p/r person will take your horse's temperature, pulse and respiration. The readings will probably be higher than normal from the excitement and the trip. I've had my horse check in with a pulse of 80—after standing in line 20 minutes. With experience the horses learn to relax and take all the nonsense in stride. If his temperature is much higher than normal, your horse might be ill, and you could be asked to come back for another check later.

The veterinarian will spend about five minutes examining your horse and making notes on the rider card about problems and peculiarities. At this time you will declare any points you wish to have noted, such as a scrape received in the trailer, a ticklish back, splints, windpuffs, and so forth. This way there will be no doubt about what happened during the ride, and what happened beforehand, an important point should you be eligible for best-condition judging.

He might check the feet, looking for problems and the quality of the shoeing job. The feet should be cleaned beforehand. After a thorough examination, you'll be asked to trot the horse out, in a figure eight or straight ahead. This is to check for lameness and observe the way of going. A funny mover will have that noted on his card.

By the way, if the horse does not trot, you'll be asked for the equivalent gait. It's a good idea to teach your horse to move out freely before the ride, or else have someone run along behind him to make him go. A very stubborn horse might have to be ridden.

If your horse fails the vet exam for some reason, or there is some doubt about his condition, you can usually bring him back for a recheck in a few hours. If he's just a little off, a short ride might loosen him up.

After the vet has okayed your horse to start, someone will use a livestock marking crayon to write his number on both hips. Your horse may kick at this the first time or two, so watch him. The number is usually drawn in a contrasting color, so if you plan to go to a horse show the following week, try and get a more subtle shade. The numbers are hard to get off, and you'll see many horses wearing four or five faded numbers after a few rides. The hip numbers are easily read during the ride, and allow for the identification of a loose horse. When so many horses are the same color, physical description and name aren't sufficient.

Pre-Ride TLC

After all this is done, tack up and take the horse for a short ride, perhaps two miles or so. Familiarize him with the trail, and what's going to be on it. It's a good idea to have a look at the last part of the trail; if you should be racing in, you'll know of potential hazards.

After you've ridden a ride a time or two, you'll be familiar with the trail, and can plan better strategy. For now, just get your horse used to the country. Don't get him hot, and don't risk injury.

Upon your return, put the horse up for the night, blanketing him if it is the least bit chilly. You will be starting out very early, and you don't want the horse to be stiff. By now the horse should have had a good drink of water, but don't get too upset if he refuses to drink. Try letting him drink from a creek, if there is one, or with other horses, or hold the bucket up to his mouth. When he gets really thirsty, he'll drink. After a ride or two he'll learn to drink water, wherever he finds it, whatever the flavor.

If tomorrow's ride is a 50-miler, give the horse half his normal grain ration tonight, with all the hay and water he wants. He can eat all night, and you can give him a little more at 4 A.M. if you like. Keep any late feedings small, since you want him to run empty. If the ride is a 100-miler, the horse needs full rations to keep him going.

Dose him with electrolytes, using a clean wormer syringe. Use pancake syrup or molasses to make a thin paste with the suggested dosage of electrolyte. Syrup works better, since it flows in any temperature, while molasses is like concrete in cold temperatures.

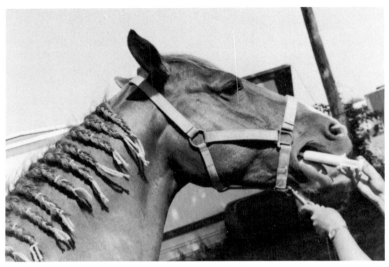

Whether the horse likes it or not, "shooting" the electrolytes down his throat with a clean wormer syringe is efficient and fast. You know exactly what went in.

Two ounces of syrup and an ounce of electrolyte, depending on the formula, is usually an adequate dose. Don't overdo it. More is not better; it's worse.

Electrolytes can be put in the feed or water, and this may work fine at home, but your horse is no dummy, and he isn't going to touch the stuff out here. After all, he's had all sorts of awful things happen to him today, and now you're trying to poison him. It's better to squirt the dose down his throat quickly and leave him alone. If he absolutely won't stand for that, sneak a small amount into his grain with a glop of molasses.

If he refuses to eat, try spoiling him with a few cut carrots or apples. Sometimes a companion horse that eats well will encourage a stubborn eater, and you might even let the other horse steal his feed. Jealousy sometimes works. If nothing works, leave him alone.

While you leave him in peace, check your tack for the morning;

make sure everything is handy, and that you did not forget anything. Actually your checklist should have kept you from leaving without something vital, but if you did, borrow or buy another. Make sure that you have clean pads and protective tubing.

Packing for the Ride

If you plan to carry a banana bag or something of the sort, pack it now with your small essentials. Keep them to a minimum, as you'll be busy all day and won't have time to use most of it. A chapstick, an orange or other small munchie, salt tablets if you use them, a hoof pick, a collapsible cup, a pocket knife, a leather thong and an Easyboot will take care of most of your needs. You might not even want that much. Few riders carry water; hence, the cup. It's more sanitary than slurping from your hand, and faster. If you suspect you'll be out after dark, have a flashlight and spare batteries available. Don't carry them around all day; pick them up at camp or one of the later checkpoints. A ride checklist is included in Appendix D.

Secure your sponge, towel or scoop to your saddle with buckle straps or tie strings. Hundreds of sponges are lost every year because they aren't tied securely. A banana bag can be strapped to the front of an English saddle, or the cantle of a stock-type saddle. You can also use a biker bag, a small nylon bag that will fasten to your belt, or to the two small dee rings on the right side of the English saddle. It has the advantages of being small, washable and cheap.

After you've decided what to carry with you, line out what should go to the checkpoints. The big five-gallon buckets that you can get at a bakery for a dollar or two are perfect for this, since they usually have lids. Write your name on the lid, and the checkpoint it is destined for, such as Hollander #1, Hollander #2, and so forth.

Inside the bucket should be spare towels or sponges, electrolytes, a bit of grain, an Easyboot, and your lunch, depending on which check you're preparing for. Even if you have no crew, you can send the buckets out with the vet or ride staff, and they'll be waiting for you when you arrive.

In most situations crewing for yourself is more efficient, but it is nice to have help and information about the other riders. A crew, one or more, is always glad to see you after a long day. If you haven't a crew, consider a dog. They are always happy to see you, and have no questions about where you've been all this time. In a high-humidity climate you'll have to have a crew to spray the horses down and cool them at the checks.

Spare shoes should be included in your supplies. An Easyboot will get you into camp, and the ride farrier, or yourself, can replace the missing shoe. This is the perfect sport for veterinarians and horse shoers; they can save money by doing most of the work themselves. Don't forget to include spare pads if you use them.

The ride meeting is usually held about dark, and will inform you about the route, and any problems that exist. The rules will be laid out, and completion time will be announced. This is the time to make your feelings heard if you dislike one of the rules, or consider it unfair, but don't be obnoxious about it. Sometimes these things are changed, sometimes not.

The veterinarians will define the pulse and respiration criteria to be met throughout the ride, the length of stops, and the length of time allowed for recovery. If your horse doesn't recuperate within that time limit, he'll be pulled. Someone will tell you where the water is to be found, and other pertinent facts. Sometimes maps are available.

While on the ride, you'll be able to use ointments and salves on injuries, such as galls, and electrolytes and cooling washes at your own discretion. However, you won't be allowed to use stimulants, tranquilizers, analgesics or anti-inflammatory drugs. If in doubt, ask the vet. If necessary in a life-threatening situation, he will treat the horse. After the final post-ride check, you'll be able to treat the horse with whatever you feel is needed.

What to Wear

As soon as your horse and tack are taken care of, you can decide what to wear. Starting at skin level, long underwear or pantyhose will protect you from pinching and chafing. Tights last longer than pantyhose, and are favored by Ride-and-Tie competitors, who wear them under running shorts (more about that later). This can result in some outrageous color combinations. If you have a tough hide, you can manage without them.

When you ride fast for a long time, especially when posting, jeans tend to ride up your leg and bunch in painful wrinkles at your knees. This can actually turn them black and blue, with perhaps a tint of red. Ace bandages used as knee wraps help protect your knees and keep your jeans smoothed out. Pant clips, like those used in saddle-seat riding, can also keep the cuffs down where they belong. You can wrap the cuffs with duct tape which is effective but messy. English breeches are another option, since they are tapered to prevent riding up. A few wear sweat pants, since they are soft and comfortable.

As for footgear, running shoes are the most popular, since they are best for running alongside the horses. A few wear western boots, hiking boots, and English riding boots. One advantage of high boots, particularly rubber ones, is leg protection—no pinching from the stirrup leathers, and they allow you to wade right into a creek to wash your horse down. Of course, if you don't mind coating your running shoes with muck and squishing about in it for the remainder of the day. . . . High boots can be hot, but they make it easier to stay on a snorty horse early in the morning, and you can change at the lunch stop. You can wear breeches or jeans with boots, wrapping the excess material to the outside of your leg.

Don't wear jeans with a heavy inseam, and make sure they are well broken in on training rides before wearing them to an endurance ride. If you choose the wrong clothing, you could suffer a long time before getting a chance to change.

When you are using an English saddle, and choose not to wear boots, slip fleece nosebands over the stirrup leathers to prevent pinching. This is especially important in ride-and-tie competition when you are wearing running shorts.

Above the waist, it doesn't really matter what you wear, but remember that halter and tank tops can give you one heck of a sunburn; t-shirts are better. If you prefer the other, a coat of sunscreen is a good idea. Don't wear a heavy jacket unless it is very cold; wear a light jacket, vest and long-sleeved shirt, making layers that can be shed at successive checkpoints. That way you'll be comfortable as the day warms up. It's surprising just how warm riding makes you. You may want to send a jacket to the last checkpoint for use late in the day, or even a change of clothes if you suspect you might get rained on.

On your head, you should wear a cap, hat or scarf. Tennis visors don't stay on worth a darn unless they fit absolutely perfectly. Usually you'll find them scattered for the first ten miles of the trail. If you worry about losing your headgear, you can add a string, like those on the kiddy cowboy hats.

Chances are that you'll roast, but should it be cold, chaps add warmth to your legs, and a slicker will be appreciated if it rains. Weather is especially changeable in the mountains. You can arrive while it's hailing and snowing, watch it rain all night and get a sunburn during the ride.

All this advance planning is much easier if the ride is laid out in a figure-eight pattern, using camp as one of the stops. You'll have access to everything you need this way, and no crewing problems. A few rides prefer to lay out big 50- or 100-mile loops;

on those, if you forget something for one of the remote stops, you borrow or do without.

"The Last Mile"

You don't need to worry about oversleeping in the morning. Some sadist will usually blow a horn to wake everyone about 5 A.M. or so, and you can set your alarm as additional insurance.

Eat a good breakfast so that you can keep going all day. Even if you're nervous, not eating is a good way to ruin your chances of finishing. Fix your lunch, and remember that a non-carbonated beverage, like Gatorade or lemonade, sets easier on your stomach when you're riding. If you're sending anything to the checkpoints, get the appropriate bucket to the staff early. It's too late to do anything after they've left.

Apply a layer of sunscreen or suntan cream to your face for protection, making the coating thin, as you'll attract quite enough dust without it.

Start tacking up about half an hour before the start time, and plan to be in the starting area about 5 or 10 minutes early.

Put your pinney on the outside of your jacket if you wear one and check that your rider card is safe and sound. Pinning or taping the pouch opening will help prevent losing it. Remember, if you do lose it, you're out of the ride.

Clean your horse's feet one more time, and make sure he's had all the water he wants. Tighten your cinch, and tuck in all the buckle ends on your tack so that they don't come undone. You might choose to leave a halter on underneath the bridle, but it isn't necessary to carry a lead rope. Put one in your crew kit, or use stout rope reins that do double duty. Rope is comfortable to hold during a long day.

The horses at the start will be very excited, so don't get cozy with any of them and risk getting kicked. If yours kicks, a ribbon in the tail will enable you to say, "I told you so," to the unfortunate rider who cannons into you.

The Start

There are two kinds of starts—the controlled start and the shotgun start. Sometimes it is difficult to tell them apart. Ideally, everyone will move out at a medium trot or canter, gradually spreading out on the trail. Often it looks more like the clubhouse turn at Churchill Downs. Unless your horse has excellent manners, he'll be running with the rest. This is where your training pays off, as the first 10 or 15 miles are probably the most dangerous part of the ride.

Get the horse under control as soon as possible, asking for a steady trot. If he fights being rated, let him move out at his own pace for a while, then ask him to slow down. Don't waste energy doing a rodeo down the trail; let that excess energy take you someplace instead. If your horse is absolutely impossible, don't start with the rest of the pack. Let them disappear into the dust, then mount up and ride out. Or start off running on foot, forcing the horse to match your pace. Use your head!

On the Trail

The trail will be congested, and the dust thick. Much of the time you won't be able to see the ground, and will have to trust to the horse. He doesn't want to trip over a stump any more than you do.

For a first ride, plan strictly on completion, which means riding conservatively all the way. There are no trophies for being first into the first checkpoint. Everyone misjudges their horse at least once and has to poke through the final miles; it's part of the game. If you underestimated your horse, you can always speed up later on.

Don't be discouraged by all the riders passing you. You'll be surprised by how many you'll pass in the final stretch. The riders soon sift into those running to win, those running for top ten, and those who are interested in crossing the finish line sooner or later. After a few miles you can get acquainted with the people whose horses are running about like yours; you'll be spending a lot of time with them.

The ideal strategy is to go slowly for the first section, picking up the pace for the next segments, and coming across the finish line on whatever's left. That isn't always possible; a beautiful strategy can be ruined by a fractious horse. You must know your horse. If you remember only three words, let them be *know your horse!*

Don't plan to race the other riders; your main opponent is the course; your goal is to cover it as quickly as your horse is able to do so. Watch where you are going; follow the trail ribbons and keep a consistent pace; adjust for rough spots.

Matthew Mackay-Smith likens good endurance riding to driving a car. "At no point do you mash on the gas or jam on the brakes, burning out of one gait and jamming into the next." Instead, you walk up the hills rather than galloping up them, walk across the creek instead of leaping it, and so forth. He points out that you don't want to do anything suddenly; the idea is to keep your eyes open and guide the horse smoothly along the trail.

With practice, riding becomes effortless, and steering second nature. You will learn to read your horse's condition by his behavior, and know more than any centaur ever knew about his lower half. The horse should maintain the pace you ask when on level ground; if he fades to a walk of his own accord, an attitude problem is developing, and doesn't necessarily mean fatigue. Tiredness begins in the mind, so this fading may well mean that the horse *thinks* he wants to quit for a while. If possible, stop and let him eat and drink for a few minutes, refueling and refreshing his attitude.

Water the horse at every opportunity, unless the finish line is only a short distance. If he's very warm and the water cold, limit him to 10 swallows, then pull his head up for a couple of minutes. If you take every chance to water the horse, he won't tank up so heavily all at once, and that's better for him.

There will be people to open the gates for you, or simply to keep livestock in while they are open all day. If the ride manager forgot to detail a gateman, you'll have to do it yourself. It is a courtesy for all riders with you to stand and wait until you remount after closing the gate. If they went dashing off, you might never get back aboard.

Ride strategy will be discussed more thoroughly in the next chapter.

Checks and Checkpoints

Along the trail you will occasionally see someone with a clip-board, studying the riders. Yell out your number as you pass, because he's checking to see if anyone is cutting corners, and to record the progress of the riders. It can make an anxious pit crew in camp very happy to know that rider #59 just passed the last checkpoint.

During the course of the ride your horse will be examined by a veterinarian at least once, checking for signs of fatigue, and will have to pass at least two vet checks with acceptable pulse and respiration counts.

A 50-mile ride will usually have three stops, with two brief breaks of 15 minutes, and a longer lunch stop, lasting up to an hour. A 100-mile ride will have at least four mandatory stops, and probably five or six, with three long rest stops. There may also be eye checks along the route with observers watching for lameness and overstress.

The vet check is designed to protect the horses from abuse, both intentional and unknowing. It is one of the safety factors that makes endurance riding possible.

There are two basic types of stops: the mandatory stop for a specified period of time, and the stop-and-go. A stop-and-go check means that the horse may continue whenever he meets the pulse and respiration criteria, trots out sound, and has no other im-pending problems. The rider makes all the other decisions about when and where to stop; and for how long, since the clock is running all day. If you feel like taking a two-hour siesta for the

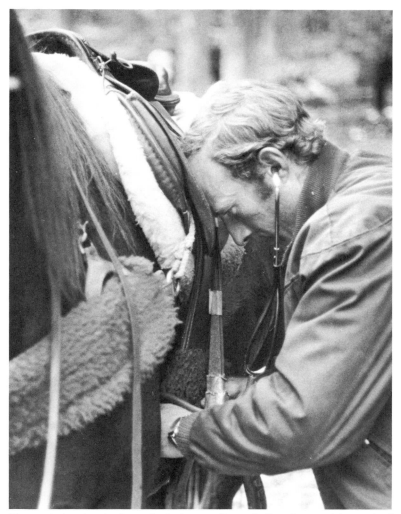

The veterinarian is there to help you through the ride and to protect your horse. He will personally have to okay your horse at each major check before you can leave on the next loop of trail.

half-way stop, that's possible, or you can move out in 20 minutes. There are advantages and disadvantages to both types of checks.

Stop and Go. A stop-and-go oriented ride is slower, and gives the riders more opportunity to use strategy. The horses are not pushed as hard, but they also don't tend to lose interest in going on during long breaks. The concept has been used successfully in rides up to 200 miles in length, and in general, the horses finish in much better condition.

The stop-and-go check was originated by Lew Hollander. While running a marathon one year he wondered what would happen if a doctor ran out and stopped all of the runners for an hour, just as the vet does on endurance rides. He realized that none of the runners would be able to continue, and wondered if horses would be better off to travel steadily and slowly through a ride, instead of fast with long stops.

He tested the idea at his own ride, the Oregon 100, and it worked great. In 1979 the Oregon 150 was run with no mandatory stops, and the riders took breaks as needed to take care of the horses and themselves. Even though the distance was unprecedented at the time, the horses felt great. At least one of them kicked up his heels and played when he got home, but it isn't on record what his rider did.

The stop-and-go check works fine as long as the riders know what they are doing. It is your own responsibility to take care of your horse with sensible riding. The horses mustn't be allowed to leave the checks without meeting the criteria, usually 64/40 in dry climates. When it's hot and humid, the respiration requirement should be waived completely, in favor of a temperature measurement.

Dr. Matthew Mackay-Smith explained why the temperature reading should be the operative one in an article that appeared in the AERC *Endurance News,* pointing out the heart has one chore, and the respiration two. The heart distributes oxygen from the lungs to the muscles, matching pulse to need. When the horse works harder than the heart can supply the needed oxygen, an oxygen debt accumulates, and when the work ceases, that debt must be serviced, through an elevated pulse. The horse will need a lot of oxygen to fill the debt, so he takes long, deep breaths.

But respiration also regulates the body temperature, along with the evaporation of sweat. Evaporation becomes ineffective in humid conditions, so panting is the only way for the horse to cool himself, once the oxygen debt is cleared up. When he switches to air conditioning instead of oxygen supply, that causes the condition of inversion, with respiration higher than pulse. Inversion is no major concern if the pulse is dropping and the body temperature is less than 104°.

When air temperature and humidity together total over 140, the fit horse will show fast pulse recovery, and an early shift from slow, oxygen supplying breaths to panting, perhaps over 100 breaths a minute. It means that he took care of his oxygen debt promptly and is now cooling his body. If he is artificially cooled with large amounts of water and ice, he'll stop panting.

The horse under more stress will show nearly equal pulse and respiration readings, such as 72/72, and that means he is having a hard time taking care of a large oxygen debt, and isn't cooling himself down. If a strict 64/40 requirement is adhered to, the fit horse will be penalized because he is panting, and the soft horse will go out on the trail, still struggling to recover. Forced cooling stops the panting, but is hard on the horse. Checking the temperature would eliminate any doubts as to the condition of the horse.

The nature of a stop-and-go check encourages riders to ride more slowly through a ride, planning to hit the checks with a recovered horse. The mandatory check, on the other hand, encourages the competitive riders to come racing in with a fatigued horse, knowing they'll have that 15 minutes or more to get the pulse and respiration back down. If they don't come in fast, they get left behind by the other riders, and it can be hard to make up a minute or two when everybody is going fast. So, a hot horse comes in and stands around, and that isn't good for him.

The mandatory stop also encourages a type of race fever, beginning when an unknowing rider allows a soft, unfit horse to race with the tough front runners. The horse is game enough to stick with them all the way to the checks, and there he gets his breath back, just in time to go dashing out again. But the pace is just too much for him—he's the one that goes down with exhaustion later on.

Stop-and-go checks discourage this by sifting out the fit horses and sending them on down the trail. The marshmallows have to wait for full recovery, and their riders get a good chance to think. Next time the marshmallow horse will be in better shape; this time he'll finish without hurting himself.

You will be timed into each stop, and that time will be noted on your rider card. Your horse might be checked immediately for a pulse and respiration count, or you may be allowed to wait until the horse is recovered. The vital signs coming into a stop are not nearly so important as the check before leaving, as a horse can come in with extremely high pulse and respiration, yet recover to reasonable levels in a short time. But, if he doesn't recover, it would be risky sending him back out.

Speeding the Recovery

If the horse is checked immediately on arrival, he will be re-checked before leaving. Meanwhile you can give your horse a drink and a wash. The length of the check will determine what you do. At a stop-and-go check, you can leave whenever you are ready and your horse is okayed. At a mandatory check you'll have to wait the full period before leaving.

A 15-minute check gives you time to water the horse and wash his face, lower legs and neck. If you use a towel to wash the horse down with, drape it over his neck for additional cooling while you check the shoes. Let the horse eat whatever interests him. Grass is the best at this time, since it is palatable and moist, making it easily digested. The girth should be loosened and the stirrup run up, or hung over the seat, reminding you not to leave without tightening the girth again. This also makes it easy for p/r checkers.

Don't soak a horse that will have to stand around. If he came in hot, cool him out to keep him loosened up. This may slow his recovery slightly, but will be better for him. This is especially important if the horse is slightly off and might stiffen if he stands too long. Did you ever sit down after working hard and feel like you just couldn't move a muscle? That's the way the horse feels, and that's why the stop-and-go check works so well. The horse comes in cooled out and nearly recovered, and can relax during the stop. When he's ready, he can go.

Be especially careful to keep cold water off of the large muscles, as this can provoke severe stiffening, literally "tying up" the horse. This isn't the same as azoturia, however.

If the day is hot and humid, the procedure is slightly different. You must wash the horse down frequently, and this is where a good crew comes in handy. They'll meet you at various points along the trail and wash the horses down with a sprayer. At the stop, if it is necessary to meet strict respiration requirements, the horse gets drenched with cold water everywhere but the hindquarters, and ice is applied to the legs and the jugular vein. The horse is kept moving to prevent siffening.

The Hour-Long Stop. If you've got an hour-long stop, you have plenty of time to take good care of the horse. Strip him of tack and let him eat hay or grass, plus a small amount of grain if he wants it. Make sure he has some bowel sounds before letting him have any grain, and don't even consider grain if he's colic-prone.

The horse must go back to the vet in 30 minutes for a recheck that will determine whether or not he can continue the ride. Meanwhile you can clean him up a bit and grab a bite to eat for yourself.

Keep an eye on the horse but give him a chance to relax. There is such a thing as taking too much care of him. Walk him around every few minutes to keep him from stiffening, and make sure he has all the water he wants.

He'll probably urinate during a long stop, and that's a good sign. Observe the color, and if it is darker than the usual straw yellow, let the vet know when you are checked again. If he's trying, but can't, let him eat and drink at will until he does.

Keep him blanketed during the stop if it is the least bit chilly, or at least throw something over his hindquarters. This is especially important in cold, rainy weather. He might appreciate having his legs massaged, but he will probably prefer to be left alone. If a creek is handy, let him stand in it for a few minutes to take the heat out of his feet and legs.

If possible, lay out a fresh, clean saddle pad and girth cover. This isn't a life or death matter, and you can let the first set dry in the sun while you wait, but a clean set helps prevent sores and galling, and probably feels much better to the horse.

Keep the horse quiet, locating a shady spot if you can. During a short stop you'll want to stay close to the vet and p/r staff, since you want them to come to you promptly when it's time for a check. That way you don't risk the pulse going back up again. It helps if you aren't standing too close to the trail, and are away from the excitement, but that isn't always possible. Checks early in the ride usually look like a traffic jam. The biggest danger is in being kicked, or your horse kicking someone.

If there is a crowd at the water trough or creek, water your horse promptly and move away for a few minutes, then return. Don't hog the entire area, and don't wash him down in the water trough. That fouls the water for everyone else. Dip your sponge or towel in a bucket if possible, or at least try to get a minimum of crud in the main water supply.

If you are on a 15-minute break, get your horse okayed to continue about five minutes before it's time to go. In an hour stop, you'll return at the 30-minute mark for a recheck. The veterinarian will be looking at a number of things to determine just how tired your horse is.

The Vet Check. Pulse and respiration aren't the only indicators of condition; at times they are deceiving, and the other signs of fatigue will tell the real story. The person in charge of the check should always be authorized to pull or hold any dubious horses for a few minutes longer, as the entire purpose of the vet check is to protect the horses.

Muscle tone is one of the indicators, and the vet will look for signs of cramping and stiffening, and small tremors in the large muscles.

The skin pinch test will check for dehydration. Grasp a fold of skin and pull it away from the neck, then release it. A horse that is fully hydrated will have the skin flatten almost immediately, but a horse that is seriously dehydrated will not lose the fold at all. Some dehydration is present if the fold remains for three seconds or longer. True dehydration will be accompanied by little or no saliva, sunken, dry eyes, and lack of sweat. Some horses have poor skin reactions under normal conditions, and this should be determined at the pre-ride examination.

Gut sounds are another important indicator of fatigue. A rested horse will have nearly constant gurgling and splashing noises in the abdomen, from the activities of digestion. As the horse tires during a ride, blood is diverted from the gut to the survival organs, which are the brain, heart, lungs and muscles. This slows the gut down, and when the horse is totally exhausted, it will shut down altogether. If you are in doubt about whether the horse should have grain or hay during a ride, listen to his gut with a stethoscope for signs of activity before any feeding. If all's quiet, let the vet know.

Capillary refill time is checked by pressing a finger against the gum, leaving a white spot. The number of seconds required for that white spot to turn pink again, indicating restored circulation, is the capillary refill time. Normally it takes less than three seconds, but may take up to ten if the horse is heavily stressed. The membranes will congest and darken, showing that the horse is having trouble handling the byproducts of fatigue in his body. The eyes may also be bloodshot (injected).

The anal sphincter response will be tested with the poke of a finger, and if it is totally relaxed, the horse is severely fatigued.

Diarrhea, or scours, also indicates stress, and can be caused by improper diet. If the horse has lost all interest in feed and water, or wants to roll, colic may be developing, or he might be very tired.

When you trot out, the vet will watch for lack of coordination and any interfering, plus lameness. A horse reluctant to move out may just need a few more minutes of rest, or may be totally worn out. You have to look at the entire horse.

If the horse doesn't meet all criteria, he will be rechecked in 10 minutes. If he isn't recovered within another half hour or so, he will usually be withdrawn from the ride.

When your card has been signed, and your time is up, you're free to go. A green horse may not be especially delighted with the idea; that makes it especially nice to have a companion at this time. Make sure that you have your rider card securely tucked away, and that the timer marked your time out on it.

Back on the Trail

Most endurance rides plan checks every 12 miles or so. If the overall distance of a ride seems overwhelming, think of it in those short increments, from check to check, and it won't seem quite so difficult. Remember, the horse can't read or count, so he doesn't know how far it is.

A steady trot covers the most territory, but you should change gaits to relieve the monotony and conform to the terrain. Walk or tail up the hills and trot down them if you choose, taking advantage of the law of gravity. A few people dismount and run ahead of the horse on downhill stretches, saying it saves time and saves the forelegs as well. In fact, you could tail uphill, run down-hill, and ride on the flat stretches.

Pace your horse at seven to eight miles an hour for completion; start conservatively and speed up in the final quarter if the horse is up to it. If you ride too slowly, such as a four-mile-an-hour

One of the easiest ways to conserve your horse's energy is to dismount when climbing hills. If he refuses to tail and tow you along behind him, you must lead him, as this rider is doing. A formidable hill will leave you pretty wobbly, but the horse would feel even worse if he had to carry you as well.

walk, the horse will not benefit from the elastic rebound of the faster gaits, in which he bounds from leg to leg. At a walk, each foot gets picked up, one at a time, just like a human has to do, and that can be a tough chore after a while. The horse may get very bored and want to quit, and then you really get nowhere. Moseying along carrying heavy weight is harder than chugging along at a nice trot and getting the job done promptly.

You can alternate gaits by the clock, cantering three minutes and trotting five. If your horse isn't up to that, trot five and walk three. While walking you may prefer to get off and walk yourself, as you both travel the same speed. You'll also be less stiff and sore after the ride if you walk for a few minutes every hour or so.

During your first ride, the final segment is the toughest, and riding alone at this point can be quite depressing. It gives you too much time to wonder why you're out here in the boondocks on a tired horse. The tired horse will also spark up and move out if he has some company. Horses are herd animals and dislike being left behind.

Some people enjoy racing in the last mile or so, and that can be a tremendous psychological lift after a long, slow ride. There aren't many who can pass up such a challenge. Just use good sense, for it isn't worth risking two necks for 48th place instead of 49th. Running a tired horse is risking injury, especially on rough ground.

Crossing the line is a big relief, and the timer will take your card immediately. The horse may be checked immediately, and you'll be asked to return in 30 minutes for a recheck.

While you're caring for the tired horse, start planning your next ride. Don't evaluate all rides according to the one you just finished, which might seem like the dumbest thing you ever did. The next rides will be much, much easier, and you'll feel more like partying after the ride instead of sleeping.

Besides, there are bigger challenges ahead, such as your first 100-miler, and the 150-mile and longer distances.

6: How Far Ahead Are the Next Riders?

NOW THAT YOU'VE HAD a look at the basic endurance technique, it's time to look at the tricks of the trade and the finer points of strategy. Depending on your interests, this chapter can make it easier to complete a ride perhaps a little faster, and who doesn't want to go faster?

Some people are only interested in completion, and that's okay. After all, as we said earlier, the basic premise of endurance riding is *To complete is to win.* But there are always people who aren't content to merely ride through—they want to race. It may not be a case of "My horse is better than yours," but of "My strategy is better than yours." A clever rider can take an average horse to top placings, while a poor one might not even finish the ride, even if he's mounted on the best of the bunch.

If winning is your goal, you have to work hard and totally devote yourself to the sport, physically and mentally. You can even get to the point where finishing second is a let-down—you rode hard all day and did your best, and it just wasn't good enough. There's nothing wrong with wanting to win as long as you remember who's doing most of the work, and remember to take good care of him. All the wins in the world aren't worth the sacrifice of a good horse.

The first point to be learned in successful endurance riding is that the horse is the important half of the partnership, and that the rider is expendable, even if he is the brains of the outfit.

ENERGY: THE ESSENTIAL INGREDIENT

Think of your horse as having a bucketful of energy at the beginning of the ride. That energy comes from the feed he eats, and is expended in body maintenance and transportation. While the horse

99

works, the bucket is slowly refilled from the digestive process, unless the horse reaches total exhaustion, in which case digestion shuts down almost entirely.

What takes more energy? Carrying a rider up a hill, or towing him with the tail? Riding along at a walk, or walking alongside the horse? If the second option of both those questions was not your choice, then you're more interested in preserving yourself than your horse.

At the beginning of the day, you start with a full bucket of energy and when that bucket's drained, for all intents and purposes, you're washed up for the day. If you're not careful, you'll be one of those walking in, towing a tired horse. If you are careful to conserve the energy of the horse, or to ride slowly throughout the day, or to run yourself instead of the horse, you might cross the finish line with a generous portion remaining in the bucket. Those leftovers could put you a few places higher, if that's what you want.

Rest stops during the course of the ride will refill the bucket slightly, and help you go long distances, but most of the energy comes from the final pre-ride feeding. In a 50-mile ride, you should run the horse fairly empty, as the distance is short and the pace fast. In a ride that's 100 miles or more, the horse needs to start fairly full, and should get a few chances to eat along the way in order to keep going.

STRATEGY: KEY TO WINNING

In endurance riding, time is also energy. If you save a few seconds here, and a minute there, whether through not missing that obscure turn of the trail, or being more efficient in caring for the horse during the stops, it all adds up. Most endurance races are won by seconds, and it can be very hard to make those seconds up at the very end of the ride. The more "strategy" time you save, the less energy you will have to use up, for going fast drains the bucket more quickly than going slow. Or you may choose to ride fairly fast, then give the horse rest stops, letting him graze for a few minutes, or pausing for an hour or two on lengthy rides to recharge.

Obviously, it's harder to figure out strategy for a ride with mandatory stops of set lengths. Stop-and-go checks turn the ride into a large outdoor chess game—a real game, instead of a trail ride. The primary challenge is in getting over the trail at the fastest speed that your horse can safely manage; beating the other riders is purely secondary. You don't race the competition until the end is near, and at that time, if there's someone to race with, you can issue a challenge. It is pure foolishness to begin racing the others at the start. Instead, concentrate on getting maximum performance from your horse. If you got the best performance from your horse that he could manage, you've won in a way that many never do. If that best is 99th place, that's an accomplishment, and you can be proud.

There are various ways to get the utmost from your horse, and that is where the strategy comes in. Some people choose to run much of the way with their horses; others only dismount for tailing uphill. Knowing the horse thoroughly allows you to choose an efficient pace that covers the country with a minimum of physical effort, and it tells you when he needs to stop and rest along the way. Ignoring what the horse is telling you is a sure way to destroy any chance you may have to win or place. If you're really aggressive about helping your horse, you'll cross the finish line in a state of exhaustion—and satisfaction.

Planning strategy begins well before the ride. You can psych both yourself and your horse for a top effort. When you spend a lot of time with a horse, you develop a tremendous empathy, responding to changes in mood and attitude in a mirror-like fashion.

The 1979 national champion endurance horse, Law Thunder, certainly had that type of relationship with his owner, Hanne Hollander. The week before each ride, Hanne went out and talked to Thunder every night, telling him that he was going to have

Holly Gervais, 1979 national junior champion, demonstrates tailing uphill behind her stallion, Tezero. Apparently Tezero steers with his tail, but most people use a long line attached to the bit for guidance and control.

to put out a big effort on the following Saturday, and to try to win. According to Hanne, Thunder told her he could do this, and made a promise to win.

She considers it important for a horse to make this type of promise, and believes that the horse won't want to break it, bravely fighting off opposition at the end of the ride in order to keep his promise. During 1979 Thunder kept his promises very well, winning seven out of nine starts at distances ranging from 50 to 200 miles.

Perhaps you feel silly talking to your horse. Perhaps he's embarrassed to be seen speaking to you in front of his friends. The point is that both the horse and the rider can by psyched up for a race, just as a rodeo rider convinces himself that no bronc can throw him.

Planning the Ride

Plan the ride before you start, noting terrain and footing all the way, plus any possible problems from the weather. You know your horse's strengths and weaknesses better than anyone else does. As Dr. Matthew Mackay-Smith puts it, "You sit down and figure out how fast you can go over that course under these conditions, and see how close you can come to it during the actual ride."

Boyd Zontelli and his family demonstrate that endurance riding is really a family affair, as they tail up a hill in tandem. Everyone learns to cooperate!

The footing at a ride will determine just how fast you can go most of the time. For example, you can ride at a brisk gallop on wet sand without tiring the horse very much, but loose, dry sand will quickly wear him down. In addition, the risk of injury is very high.

He continues, "If your horse is as good as you think he is, and you are smart as you think you are, you will come up exactly where that horse belongs. The only horses in front of you will be better horses with smarter riders . . . the people who are doing the very best job get the most out of their competitive efforts, bringing them somewhere near the front. If you see a horse that is winning all the time, you can be sure that he has great talent, that he is well prepared and intelligently ridden. You can also bet that there are probably three or four people somewhere behind him who could have been there for the finish if they had ridden their ride instead of his."

To plan effectively, you must be familiar with the trail, whether from previous years, or by pre-riding it on a spare horse, or even a motorcycle. If nothing else, this helps keep you from getting lost and wasting time and energy.

Plan to work the horse at a constant energy, defined by Mackay-Smith as a consistent output of energy to produce forward motion, but not necessarily a steady speed. If the trail is steep, slow the horse down to maintain that constant energy use, rather than making him work harder to chug up the hill at his working pace. He points out that many people believe it is easier to run uphill than down, and pace their horses accordingly. You must rate the horse; if he's smarter, you should carry him through the ride!

If you are a heavyweight rider, you must plan your strategy to compensate for that, and you'll probably spend more time on the the ground than the average lightweight. Try to plan a time schedule for the ride, but don't make it an ironclad rule to be at point A at 8:15 A.M. and point B at 9:23 A.M. Horses do not run like trains, and should you find yourself behind your schedule at some point, don't try and make up all the lost time in one mad dash. Instead, move out a little faster, making up the time steadily and efficiently.

The Start. There are two different strategies for starting a ride; one is to start slowly, allowing the horse to gradually get in the swing of things and become fully efficient. The other is to move out and get out away from the pack, justified by the number of accidents that occur early in the ride. If you are in front, you get no dust, and you're not expected to pick up the pieces if someone has an accident. The horse can see where he is going, and you can easily pick out the ribbons.

On the other hand, laying back and letting the pack vanish into the dust works well for many people. You can always figure that a lot of folks will want to race from the word go, and they'll make mistakes along the way. Meanwhile, you move steadily along, missing none of the turns and losing only a little bit of time. Often the leaders come dashing back, having missed the trail and gone haring off into the wilderness.

In choosing a starting strategy, consider your horse. Does he like to start slowly and improve during the day, or is he a chameleon that matches his pace according to the competition and stays where you put him? Does he like to run up front and stave off opposition from behind, or is he better off moving up late in the ride, making up time when everyone else is flagging? This is your decision, right or wrong. If you do wish to start slowly, will your horse accept that, or will he waste more energy crowhopping and rearing? If that's the case, you might as well move out and cover some country. Some horses are good enough to be able to run 10 miles before being rated; others will plod the entire day if allowed to do that.

The First Leg. Saving the energy stores in your bucket should start early in the ride, with the first hill, whether it be a mile from the start or 20 miles out. If the first of the ride is the roughest, it's senseless to go out and sprint through it.

Dr. Mackay-Smith tells of a ride in New York, a 100-miler that led off with the ruggedest 50 miles imaginable. According to him, the fastest you could cover that first section was 11 hours. The last 50 miles could be covered in a little over four hours—if you had saved enough horse. Some people had tried to race through the rugged section, and consequently had nothing left at the end. They ran out of gas at the 75-mile point, and the Mackay-Smiths went on to win.

Many riders don't start conserving energy until the horse gets tired; by that time, it's too late to do much good. You only have one bucketful of energy to work with. The easiest way to conserve energy is to dismount and run alongside the horse whenever he is going slowly enough. If he's walking, you can do the same, and if you're in shape, even jog along at a fair pace. If you choose to sit in the saddle at a speed slower than you yourself can run at, you aren't being very helpful.

Most opportunities to run with the horse come in rugged terrain, where there are a lot of rocks, or on steep trails. You should do a little conditioning of your own during the training period in order to be ready. If it's possible to ride faster than you can run, then climb aboard and go.

The rule in training is to ride uphill, building up the horse's strength, and to run downhill, saving concussion on the forelegs. In racing, you get the most for your efforts by tailing up the hills, running behind the horse at a jog, and riding down the hills, unless it is too steep. Tailing at the trot does take some training, and you must be able to control the horse. However, it does get you to a hilltop very quickly without wearing the horse out.

Pacing Your Horse. In the first part of the race, whether you chose to lag or dash well ahead, you must get the horse settled into an efficient pace as soon as possible. As soon as the horses string out on the trail, you can adjust your pace without fear of being run over or into. However, it takes 10 to 15 miles for the horse to warm up thoroughly and go into his most efficient phase of operation.

Marathon runners feel that you should start slowly, letting your body increase the energy output smoothly and steadily. This postpones "hitting the wall," a phenomenon experienced by both runners and horses. Hopefully it will postpone it to a longer distance than you have to go, or at least allow you to get farther. However, there's a vast difference between people in running togs and a bunch of high-powered, well-fed horses on a cool morning, all trying to get on one little trail.

Your optimum pace should be faster than your competitors if possible, but it will vary according to the horse's attitude, the competition, the weather, the length of the haul yesterday, and a multitude of other things that concern the horse. In training you should have established a comfortable freewheeling pace that needed no urging or holding back, and it should be a pace the horse enjoys. If he's pulling, let him speed up a little; if he's lagging, you may have the start of a physical problem, or merely an attitude problem. You must be able to read the horse and decide which it is. If you urge him on when he needs rest, you'll blow the entire day.

If he seems sluggish at a brisk trot, jump off and run along with him for a quarter mile or so before remounting. If this improves him, you were going just a little too fast, wearing him out. If it doesn't change anything, speed him up and try to awaken his interest.

While running alongside, have a look at his legs, looking for injuries and counting the shoes. This is a great opportunity to see how everything's going down there, and you can see if he's traveling a little off. Lameness is easily spotted, though not so easily diagnosed. The horse might have bumped a shin on a stump, or he might have bruised a foot. If he does have an injury, you've got to decide whether it would hurt him to continue.

A minor bruise would allow you to walk on through the ride, but a cracked coffin bone or pulled tendon could be damaged beyond repair if you went on. If you suspect a problem, walk into the next vet stop and have an expert make the decision.

If the horse is slightly off in one foot, keep him in the opposite lead or diagonal. He'll try and keep most of his weight off of it, but if it is just a cramp, it'll work out. You have to be the first to know of any problems, and take action on them immediately. The veterinarian at the stop shouldn't surprise you with information that was available on the trail.

Riding alone is the best way to rate your horse, since he isn't influenced by the other horses. In company he may go faster than he should, or slower than necessary. This makes it hard to read his energy level, for some horses love racing and will run themselves into the ground to stay competitive. Other horses couldn't care less about the whole idea, and you'll have to push them every step.

If you're riding for time, gravity can be your best friend. If you don't believe it, try running downhill on your own two feet. With practice you'll find a rate of speed that takes little muscular effort to maintain, and causes only a slight amount of concussion to bother you.

With a bit of practice your horse can achieve the same, unless his conformation is just not suited to it. Some horses can never manage more than a walk or slow jog on hills; others float in perfect balance.

On the flat, a trot is the most efficient gait, but you should change gaits occasionally to use different muscles. Dr. Mackay-Smith acknowledges that human marathoners prefer to maintain a steady pace, but points out that a human cannot maintain his gait by elastic rebound, as the faster gaits of the horse do. Constant muscular repetition gets the man where he's going; spring action makes the horse go. After a while tension and boredom interfere with that spring action, and a change to the canter for a short distance will loosen the horse up once more. Dropping to a walk will allow you to check his way of going, and for signs of fatigue that are more obvious at a slow pace.

Estimate Your Speed. Learn to "feel" how fast you are traveling by riding measured distances and recording the time it takes. You can usually estimate mileage from good maps, or drive the route in a vehicle. Interval work on a race track will also give you a sense of pacing, an essential for good strategy. Table 3 on the next page shows how to convert traveling time on a measured distance into miles per hour.

When to Rest—and How. If the horse is weaving all over the trail and it's becoming hard to balance on him, he could use a few minutes of rest. If nothing else, it will improve his attitude toward going on. One way to determine how fatigued the horse may be is to grab his tail and pull it towards you. If you can swing his entire rear around, he's probably worn out. If he resists the pull, there's some energy left in your bucket. A look at his vital signs will tell you more.

You have to realize that every horse has his strong and weak points in endurance riding; some can make better time on the uphill stretches, others are unbeatable going downhill. Your horse might be unbeatable on the flat, but few rides are totally flat. If that's the case, you have to plan your ride in order to get him to the front, ready to race when it's time to do so. It's useless to race to the first check.

Watch where you're going. A tired horse is more prone to

Table 3
ESTIMATING SPEED

MINUTES PER MILE	MILES PER HOUR
15	4.0
14	4.3
13	4.5
12	5.0
11	5.5
10	6.0
9	6.5
8	7.5
7	8.5
6	10.0
5	12.0
4	15.0
3	20.0
2	30.0

stumbling and possible injury, and it takes more energy to scramble through a rock pile than to go around. Watch the riders ahead of you; don't gawk at the scenery and crash into someone giving their horse a well-earned drink.

Ideally, the middle part of the ride should be where you gain the most time, using the horse's energy wisely to get him in the front. In a stop-and-go-oriented ride with no mandatory stops, using the horse intelligently becomes very important.

You prepare for the stop out on the trail. If you suspect problems are developing, stop and check the horse out for signs of fatigue. If any seem serious, walk the horse the rest of the way to the stop, allowing him to recuperate before the vet sees him. That makes a much better impression than dashing in with a weary horse; the vet will be more inclined to let you out quickly, since it's obvious that you are taking good care of the horse. You should be the first one to know how your horse feels. The vet can confirm your findings and help determine how much energy the horse still has.

In training you should have learned to determine your horse's pulse and respiration from the amount of work being done, without having to make a count by the watch. This skill will serve you well in coming into a stop-and-go with a recovered horse.

For example, you estimate that you're about five miles from the stop. You rode fast for the first of the race, getting out ahead of the pack, then eased off to a steady pace for the next miles. While going a little fast, an oxygen debt has accumulated, but you've gained time on the other riders. Now you use that time, easing the horse into a slightly slower gait, from five to three miles out. This gives the horse a chance to clear his oxygen debt. While you're slowing down, everyone else is passing at will, probably crowing about beating you to the stop. Let them crow, for you have a trick up your sleeve to show them.

About a mile and a half from the stop, put the horse in an extended trot, and slow to a working trot at the mile point. Half a mile out, jump off and run in with the horse, dropping to a walk at the quarter mile mark, or approximately in sight of the check.

What you've done is ease the horse into the check, gradually lowering the pulse and respiration from their peak levels to recovery, hopefully 64/40 if you've done your homework. You're ready to go just as soon as the horse is watered, while those that passed you are still waiting.

You get out of a check quickly by coming in slowly and using a finely-honed sense of pace. The strategy begins by leaving the starting line or most recent check fast, over-riding for the first few miles to gain time. Then, as you approach the check, the pace is gradually decreased, but the heart and lungs are still working at full capacity. The heart is a pump, and a pump at high speed gets the job of clearing the oxygen debt done more quickly.

Many riders gallop until the check is only a mile away, then they walk on in. This doesn't use the pump as efficiently, and probably takes more total time than easing into the stop and leaving quickly.

The heart pump has to be kept at high speed while gradually decreasing the demands on it. The horse recovers more quickly and is ready to eat and drink immediately on arrival. That's much easier on him than running in, only to stand around and wait.

The vet will be impressed because the horse will look great; if there are problems, he'll be more likely to help you than pull you outright. You've proved that you have some sense, and he'll be more likely to let you out with a marginal horse than the idiot who came in at a run. Another plus for easing in comes when the horse is trotted out for a lameness check. The rest will make him look better, and he won't be stiff from coming in hot and standing.

A good stop procedure is to loosen the girth when you dismount on the way in, and to allow the horse to breathe freely. Look at his legs on the way in, and when you arrive, water him and wash the lower legs, face and neck. Check the vital signs so that you know what's going on before the vet checks him, and when he's ready, call the vet over.

If the pulse and respiration are high and you're in a hurry to leave, drenching the horse, except for the rump, will help him recover by cooling him down. But if he's over-fatigued or a little off, it could stiffen him up, making it necessary to pull him entirely.

Another trick to stop panting is to squeeze one nostril closed, forcing the horse to breath more deeply and slowly, but it doesn't deal with the basic cause—overheating.

While waiting to get out of a vet stop, keep the horse's mind on you, not the other horses. You shouldn't stand right next to the trail, as the horses going past will disturb yours. He'll want to go along, and consequently send his pulse back up. Be calm, and the horse will recover more quickly. If you're screaming at him and your crew, it's going to take a lot longer.

Getting Away Again. Keep in mind that being first into the vet stop doesn't mean first out. The Hollanders have often been behind 20 other horses when arriving, but are almost invariably the first out because they know their horses.

If you're in a mandatory stop, get your horse cared for, vetted out, and then go stand by the timer. Let them know you're waiting, and verify the time you're to leave. Compare watches and make sure they don't forget to let you out. After all, the timer is a volunteer, prone to distractions, and you don't want to find out too late that "Oh, you could have gone two minutes ago!" That's terrible for your strategy because you need to make it up, going faster than optimum to catch up.

Don't wait at a vet stop for a friend; do that out on the trail. Walk into the stop and canter out if possible, since trotting might show the horse to be slightly off, and you don't want the vet to call you back. You also want to get out of sight as quickly as possible so that the next horses don't get sucked along with you.

Horses are herd animals, quite happy to stay together all day. This makes pacing harder, so you must either leave the others behind, galloping out of sight, or let them rush past. Riding alone limits the social aspects of endurance riding, but you can catch up on all the gab after the ride. Just tell the riders, "Hi," as you pass, and they won't feel too slighted.

Of course, if the horse drank a great deal of water at the stop, you're going to have to take it easy for a while. That's why you should water as often as possible in small amounts.

Passing on the Trail. When you catch up with another rider let your horse blow for a minute or two, laying back behind. When your horse is ready to go, breeze past as fast as possible and leave the other horse completely behind. If you gradually worked up on the other rider and slowly passed, his horse would probably come with you, and might even be faster than yours when it came time to race.

Instead you dash past, looking invincible with a fresh horse. Once out of sight, drop back to your most efficient pace. This can backfire if the other horse accepts the challenge and comes along.

Lew recalls riding a horse called Rainbow through the Oregon 100 one year. It is a fairly flat ride, and he had been conserving energy diligently throughout the first 65 miles. He was nearly exhausted, but Rainbow was fairly fresh when they came on the next competitor, 10 miles from camp. Lew was anxious to use his strategy, so he galloped Rainbow past. Unfortunately the other horse was also feeling pretty good and came right along. Rainbow became completely uncontrollable and ran away, all the way to the vet stop. By then he was exhausted, having emptied his bucket in one big spree. Barely clearing the vet stop, he crawled the final 25 miles, finishing the ride in 8:45. He gained most of his time in that mad sprint; it came close to eliminating him from the ride.

If you are the one being caught, instead of the other way around, then try and keep up with the passing rider. Your horse may not be able to sustain a challenge very long, but you might gain a place or two in the process. You might even hang in there long enough to race to the finish line.

Some horses prefer to run with a companion, taking turns leading the way. Two horses gaited the same can maintain a steady pace, and you won't have the mental problems that show up when a tired horse is asked to travel alone. The other rider may or may not like this; if he slows down in order to ride alone, move out and catch someone else. On the other hand, if he moves out at a speed definitely beyond your horse's ability at that time, don't hesitate to check back and stay behind. You don't want to run out of gas, and it might be possible to catch up with that horse later in the ride, after he's exhausted.

The only time to run with a faster horse is when you want to borrow some momentum long enough to catch another horse or two before easing back. If you know there is a horse just ahead that isn't much stronger than your own, but you can't quite catch up, let a stronger horse suck you along and past. Wait until the strong horse catches up, then speed up until you're satisfied with your progress, then let the strong horse go on.

Sometimes you can leapfrog a number of places in this manner and at least maintain your placing. Don't get upset about the horses passing you—they would have anyway. This way you can use a little of their strength and momentum to help yours.

If at all possible, try to open up a generous lead by the race's end. This will help prevent those last-minute sprints that can injure a horse or lose a close race. Judging from the small cloud of dust on the right side of the picture, Lew has about half a mile on the competition at this point.

The Home Stretch. If possible, build up a comfortable lead. Racing for the finish line is where many injuries occur, and you should try to avoid that. By the time you reach the home stretch, the horse will be running on heart and excitement alone, because the bucket will be drained.

If you planned it right, you and your horse might come home with a winner's trophy. Even if someone else gets there first, you should be satisfied with your achievement.

Different Rides—Different Plans

The 150- and 200-mile endurance rides made their debut in 1979 on an experimental basis. It wasn't certain whether such distance was really possible. Now we know that the horses can handle the increased distances and finish in excellent condition. The 200-mile ride will probably never be popular; there will have to be improvements made in horseshoes before it can be done on a regular basis.

The lengthy distance doesn't mean that the horse is ridden into the ground. Law Thunder, winner of the 1979 Ochoco 200, was a mile from the finish line when he spooked and refused to cross a garden hose that was stretched across the road.

Daytime temperatures must be considered in rides that are more than 100 miles long. You have the option of plugging along slowly all day, or riding fast, then giving the horse a long rest during the hottest part of the day, probably at the halfway point. A well-conditioned horse that rests during the warmest hours can often come back strong enough to catch the riders who rode steadily. You only have this option with the stop-and-go rides, however.

Night Riding

Riding at night, often necessary on rides of 100 miles or longer, is a whole new aspect of endurance riding. A skillful rider can make up a great deal of time during the dark hours, placing himself in a position to win.

It is absolutely necessary to trust your horse, since his night vision is far better than your own. They've been running around in the dark all their lives. If you don't believe this, step out some dark night and spook the horses in their pasture. They'll scamper all over the place like it was high noon, with never a false step.

This means he can go fast in the dark as long as you allow him to have his head. You will be carrying a flashlight, but you do not use it to look at the trail. That's the horse's department, and flickering a weak flashlight all over can disrupt his night vision. Reflections and shadows confuse him, slowing him down and increasing the risk of accidents. You do not need to know where the holes are, since you're on his back. Leave the driving to him!

The flashlight is only for searching for ribbons. A well-defined trail recently traveled by other horses is easy for your horse to follow. If he makes you nervous, grit your teeth and hang on.

A disposable flashlight, or a small model, with long-life alkaline batteries is good to have along. You will be using it only momentarily to check trail markers and such, but it must be dependable. When you need it, you need it badly. At daybreak you can dispose of the disposable light.

Running on foot at night is awkward since human night vision is poor. Do it only if there is moonlight that allows you to see what's ahead of you. Otherwise you risk turning an ankle or something worse, making you unable to help the horse when the sun comes up. Usually you can make better time on the horse.

During the summer, riding at night really allows you to travel. The horse won't have problems with the heat. If the other competitors are reluctant to move out, you can gain a great deal of time.

Elevator Rides

Elevator rides were developed to encourage riders to go farther with their horses, especially over 100 miles. A rider comes into the 50-mile point and has the option of continuing to the next distance, entering the 100-mile ride and dropping out of the 50, or stopping and taking the placing earned in the 50-mile division. Intentions are usually declared at arrival, but the horse must meet all criteria before continuing. If he failed to reach the 100-mile or 150-mile point, he would be completely disqualified with no miles credited at all. Elevator rides add a risk to stopping for long periods of time between vet gates, for if the horse stiffens and fails to pass the vet, you get nothing. AERC doesn't currently sanction elevator rides.

Let's look at the strategy that won the Oregon 150 in 1979 for Hanne Hollander. The only difference in elevators is that you don't know who you're competing against. The ride started at 5 A.M. Hanne escorted three juniors through the first 50 miles, which they finished 12th through 14th in overall standings. This indicates that she maintained a stiff pace, even though she was planning to do the 150. The terrain on this ride is sandy, which can be hard on the horses.

At this point she was well ahead of the other riders planning the 150, and took time for a 20-minute rest break, feeding the horse and herself. First out on the 75-mile loop, she was soon caught by Smokey Killen and Eileen Johnson. They rode together to the 75-mile mark, while Hanne tried to evaluate whether to ride the 150 or quit at 100 miles. Meanwhile, almost all the riders were getting through the stop-and-go checks quickly, and the horses were looking great. The riders had the option of choosing when and where to rest the horses, and it really helped.

Thunder got a three-hour rest break at the 75-mile point while Hanne napped. He grazed on a lead line and stayed loosened up until she was ready to go. It gave him an advantage over the horses that had gone steadily all day through the heat.

Hanne had passed two riders that were planning to do the 150 by the time she reached the 100-mile mark, so she went out immediately, just watering the horse. The 125-mile point was reached at dusk, and the cooling temperatures helped perk Thunder up. They finished in 22 hours, 2 minutes, and received best condition.

Five more riders finished the 150-miler, with times ranging from 26 hours to 27 hours, 38 minutes. The entire camp stayed up to greet them at the end.

That's one example of creative strategy in endurance racing; perhaps Thunder would have won no matter what the plan had been, but it was still impressive.

It's all part of knowing the horse, letting him rest when necessary, and covering ground when the time is right.

7: After You Cross the Finish Line

AFTER YOU'VE RIDDEN across the finish line it's time to start thinking about the next ride. How well you care for your horse now will determine how he'll do next time. The first 24 hours are critical, especially if you stressed your horse very hard.

You've been taking his vital signs all day and you know about how tired he is. A tired horse is a cranky, insistent horse. He only wants to eat and be left alone, not to walk to cool off and be brushed clean. The best thing you could do for him would be to turn him loose in a corral to relax, but that isn't always possible.

If you came in early enough to be among the best-condition candidates, you have to plan ahead for that. Usually, you will need to bring your horse back for judging two to four hours after finishing a 50, and the next morning for the 100 and longer rides. That means you'll have to undo his wraps, loosen him up again, and try to convince a crabby horse to look bright and energetic.

POST-RIDE CARE

Assuming that you rode fairly fast for the last few miles, the first item on your after-the-ride TLC list is cooling down. If the weather is hot, lead the horse around for about five minutes before loosening the girth. That gives any pinched places under the saddle a chance to recover. If you pulled the saddle off right away, a damaged area would get its circulation back all at once, stressing damaged capillaries and increasing the chance of a bad swelling.

When his breathing and pulse begin to stabilize, let him have water. If the water is really cold, don't let him have more than 10 swallows at a time; you don't want to overload an inactive

120

Boyd Zontelli asks Rushcreek Eaton for all he's got on a drive to the finish line. Eaton has a number of wins under his cinch, including the 1979 Tevis Cup in which he broke the course record. Rushcreek horses are tough competitors on the endurance trails.

stomach with a lot of chilly water. You shouldn't let him "tank up" until you are sure that there are gut sounds, indicating an active digestive tract.

Cooling Out

If the weather is chilly or windy, throw a cooler or sheet over the horse to keep him from cooling down too quickly. It's very easy for a horse to chill after a hard workout, so you must preserve his body warmth. The cooler will also absorb some of the moisture in the hair. Walk in circles so that all sides of the horse get an equal amount of sun and breeze, drying him uniformly.

Walking the horse to cool him down will let him unwind gradually and prevent stiffening. If you rode slowly throughout the ride, you probably won't have much, if any, cooling out to do.

After about 10 minutes, get the saddle off and let him roll if he wants to. Rolling will help dry him off, scratch all the itches, and massage all those tired muscles.

Cleaning Up

If it's cold out, it will be harder to get him cleaned up completely. You'll have to fold back the cooler a quarter at a time, gradually uncovering the horse so that it isn't a shock to him. You start with the neck, then the shoulders, leaving the loin area covered the longest. You'll have to brush him down a piece at a time, loosening the caked sweat and dust.

A bath is usually appreciated on a hot day, but be careful about getting cold water on the rump and loin. Scrub those areas with a damp towel if you are worried about possible tying up. Most endurance camps don't have running water, so you'll have to wash the horse with a bucket and sponge, perhaps taking the chill off the wash water with a panful of hot water. Don't use soap because it will be almost impossible to rinse the horse completely without running water.

Start with the legs, cleaning them off and checking for injuries. Work your way up the horse with your sponge.

A plastic scoop works well for washing a horse—just pour the scoopful of water down the horse as you scrub. It's a little faster than the sponge alone.

Again, check the weather. Don't fiddle around for two hours washing the horse if a storm is coming in. Get him slicked off and blanketed if needed, and do it promptly. He needs to get dried off before dark if possible, and you might need to scrub him down with a dry towel to get the job done.

Let him wander around on a lead rope to graze for about an hour. This is where the portable corrals are ideal. If you haven't got a corral, borrow a small child to lead the horse around. The horse will keep himself loosened up, and green grass is the best possible thing for him to eat. The moisture in it will help him

Portable corrals of plastic pipe are perfect for endurance horses, especially after a long ride. They can be turned loose to move about freely, and will stiffen less. Many horses also eat and drink better when loose.

recover, and it's very palatable as well as digestible. You don't want him to have grain just yet.

The horse needs to relax in the worst way from a hard day, and grazing is a natural pacifier. Watch for health problems as you care for him. Is he staring or nipping at his ribs, kicking or otherwise uncomfortable? You know him by now—does his face have an expression of pain? When you go back for your final check after the ride, ask the vet if you have any questions about your horse. That's what the veterinarian is for.

If the horse just doesn't seem right, keep a close eye on him. Don't go wandering far from the vet if you suspect problems.

Cold-Water Therapy

After the horse has had some time to unwind, he needs some cold-water therapy. A cold creek is the best place for your horse because the cold will make the blood vessels in the legs dilate, increasing circulation. That stepped-up circulation will reduce or prevent excessive swelling. The cold constricts an area at first, then causes the muscles to relax, and eases any pain.

If you can't put the horse in a creek for two hours, the next best thing is ice boots. Shipping wraps with Velcro fasteners work well for this. Fasten them on the legs, very tightly around the pastern area, loosely around the knee. Pack them with crushed ice, refilling when necessary. You can store three or four packages of ice in an ice chest until it's needed.

Three hours is enough in ice boots. If you haven't got ice, you can soak leg wraps in cold water, apply them, and resoak them every hour or so. You can also make an ice boot of inner tube that will do the job fairly well, or use buckets of cold water.

The Timetable. Your timetable reads: cool the horse out until his pulse and respiration reach near-normal levels. Clean him up and let him wander around for about an hour. Go back for your final check. Get ice boots or cold water on the legs, but be careful that he doesn't chill. Apply whichever cold-water therapy you choose for two to three hours, then apply regular support wraps.

Leg Wraps

For the support wraps you can use ace bandages alone, or track bandages over leg wraps. Non-elastic bandages should always have a wrap underneath to protect the leg. The bandages should be snug, but not too tight. If swelling appears above or below the wrappings, it's too tight. If the horse stamps and shows discomfort, check for problems.

The leg wraps will support the the tired leg and help prevent excessive swelling. They should remain on overnight. You can apply liniment, but it shouldn't be too strong, for it might blister under the heat of leg wraps. Some liniments and medications are best applied to a bare leg.

These are examples of the different kinds of protective leg wraps. The foreleg is protected with an elastic Ace bandage, suitable for exercise or support. The hindleg is fitted with a shipping wrap, padded with a felt and covered with a cotton track bandage (nonelastic). The shipping wrap is not suitable for riding, as leg strain can result.

More TLC

During the first 24 hours following a ride, the horse should have little or no grain at all. He should have all of the grass or hay that he wants, with salt available. A dose of electrolytes will help restore the body to normal.

If you are at a 50-miler, and home is near, you will probably go home as soon as possible so that the horse can be turned loose in his own pasture. Best-condition judging will interfere with that, for you'll have to wait around for hours, postponing full recovery.

If at all possible, the horse should rest overnight before being hauled home after a ride of 100 miles or more. If you only have 20 miles home, that's fine, but if you have 300 miles to go, rest the horse first.

When you get home, the horse should be turned out for several days to recuperate. Gradually build up the grain ration once more, and soak the legs about 20 minutes a day for the next week.

It takes about a month for a horse to recover fully from a hard ride. However, if you are riding through just to complete, the horse will recover enough so you can plan on a ride every two weeks, or every week if the country is easy.

Watch for lameness or other problems for several days. You shouldn't have to apologize for how he looks. If he's too thin, ease up on the work. You don't need to do much conditioning after the ride season begins, just maintenance. If you continue hard work during the ride season, you run the risk of overtraining and taking a tired horse to the ride.

8: Fatigue Is the Enemy

FATIGUE IS THE BIGGEST problem you will ever face in competition. Fatigue in a horse, as defined by Dr. Matthew Mackay-Smith, is the effect produced by use of the horse beyond his functional capacity.

A fatigued horse means that you misjudged his capacity to work in some way. All horses are different, and their bodies are also different in their capacities to withstand long-term stress. The weakest link in the chain becomes your limiting factor in competition.

For example, you might have a superbly built horse, but if his feet are of marginal quality, that is your limiting factor. The circulatory system, the lungs, or any part of the horse might be the limit you have to work with. If you don't mind riding to complete, limits are not so important. If you are interested in winning, they can make or break you.

THE WARNING SIGNS

Fatigue begins to appear as little problems with the horse. The hooves may begin to split and crush, the clinches rise shortly after shoeing, increasing pulse and tenderness, and laminitis or corns may develop. Those symptoms show that you are using them too hard, beyond their capacity.

Fatigued tendons and ligaments will thicken rapidly with soreness and filling, as opposed to the slow strengthening brought about by a proper conditioning program. Excessive work can cause chronic inflammation, setting the stage for a ruined tendon. According to Dr. Mackay-Smith, it takes a tremendous amount of stress to tear or stretch a tendon in a single event. Usually the tendon gives way from increasing stress, in the same way that mechanical fatigue in machinery gradually breaks down the parts.

127

Wind puffs are a natural occurrence in some horses and reflect the additional development brought about by hard work, done slowly over a lengthy period of time. If they are due to fatigue, they will be filled and tense.

Muscular fatigue first appears with the increased effort necessary to continue, and in decreased resilience. The horse begins to stumble and wander instead of traveling straight. The muscles will begin to twitch convulsively. Twitching might be the first sign of weariness in well-conditioned horses. It might then worsen into total contraction of the muscles, or the tying-up syndrome, that can develop into azoturia.

The most common sign of oncoming fatigue is a convulsive pumping of the heart, what Dr. Mackay-Smith describes as a "peaky pulse." This symptom appears before any problems in recovery.

Nearly all horses have a small artery just below their withers, on the side of their shoulders, which you can detect from the saddle. This artery makes it possible to take the pulse from the saddle while watering him, or while standing alongside, although on a thick-skinned horse it is hard to locate, unless he's under severe stress.

The pulse might weaken, or become persistently high. It might be very unstable, varying from minute to minute at a rest stop, usually in the range of the 60s and 70s. If the horse is moved, it might shoot up again. This means that the horse is very fatigued. You can pick out marginal horses by having them trotted a few steps. If the pulse goes from 68 to 90, you know he should be held or pulled altogether, depending on other signs of fatigue.

The horse's respiration must conform to his gait. If he gallops, he must breathe in while in the air and out when on the ground. At the trot, breathing patterns vary, depending on how the rate of foot-fall matches the need for oxygen. A long trot means he will have to delay his breathing, and a small, choppy trot makes him pant. You must try and regulate the gait to match his need for oxygen, so that he can breathe freely. If he's sighing frequently, he needs more oxygen and you should ease off the pace. An occasional skipped breath indicates that you could go faster if conditions warrant. Those skipped breaths mean that you have a little reserve in your energy bucket.

Panting indicates that he is getting overheated. Horses regulate their body temperature by direct radiation from the skin, evaporation of sweat, and air exchange through the lungs. The horse takes in cool air and breathes out hot air. This isn't an effective way to regulate temperature in humid conditions, so the horse must be cooled with large quantities of cool water. Rides in the East, South and Midwest can have this problem, making it essential, when the weather is humid, for every rider to have a pit crew ready to cool his horse at many points along the trail.

Understanding Inversion

This leads to the question of inversion, an especially sticky one in humid regions. As we have seen before, respiration is normally lower than pulse, and there are two basic needs to be supplied by it—cooling and oxygen supply. Deep breaths supply the oxygen debt and help restore the body to continue, while shallow breaths cool the horse. When the air temperature and the humidity together total more than 140, fit horses still recover rapidly in pulse rate, but shift early from oxygen breaths to cooling breaths, as many as 100 per minute or more.

Artificially cooling a panting horse will stop the panting. His body temperature might drop from 104.5° to 101°. Different horses begin panting at different body temperatures.

A dropping pulse and high respiration, known as an inversion, indicates a fit horse in hot, humid areas. This condition indicates the horse has switched over from oxygen supply to air conditioning very quickly. It means he is working well within his capacity.

In cooler areas, an inversion is usually no cause for concern. The condition will usually correct itself with rest.

In a humid area the horse with a slower recovery rate must try to replace his oxygen before cooling down; it requires slower breaths and a higher pulse to get the job done. Therefore, his body temperature will remain elevated after a few minutes of rest, instead of gradually dropping as it did with the panting horse.

A respiration recovery requirement of 40 per minute is a reasonable requirement in a low-humidity area, but when the humidity is very high, riders are forced to cool their horses very heavily to get respiration down that far. This harsh cooling is hard on the horse. Mackay-Smith suggests that pulse and temperature would be better measures to monitor under high-humidity conditions since it would give a more accurate picture of how the horse is doing. As the situation now stands, at times non-inverted horses not fully recovered are allowed to continue, perhaps into severe exhaustion, and fit horses get pulled for not "recovering" to 40.

You cannot standardize requirements for pulse and respiration for an entire nation; climatic variations must be taken into account.

Dehydration

A horse's body chemistry functions properly and most efficiently at a certain water content. Dehydration, or loss of body water, is something you must monitor during a ride, using the skin fold test. This is why you never pass up a chance to water your horse, unless it's only five miles to the finish line and you're racing.

The skin-fold test is covered in chapter 5. As dehydration worsens, the skin takes longer to flatten. A fold of neck skin will drop within two seconds under normal conditions. If dehydration is severe, the fold will take five seconds or more to relax, and may not at all.

If the horse ceases to sweat, has little saliva, and his eyes seem dry and sunken, he is severely dehydrated. Heat prostration may also be developing. This is one of the major causes of death in highly stressed horses. When the horse becomes unable to regulate his temperature, the adrenal gland becomes rapidly exhausted from trying to regulate it, and the horse will absolutely cook himself.

MORE WARNING SIGNS

The horse's digestive system reflects fatigue first in scours. The scours indicate improper diet, or lack of conditioning to handle the work, and loss of gut sounds usually follows. Some horses scour, or develop diarrhea from nerves, too. Under stress, the digestive system goes on standby while the needs of the rest of the body are taken care of. If the horse eats or drinks heavily while the system is still inactive, colic can develop.

If he fails to urinate, or if it is scant and dark, and the mucous membranes of the mouth are muddy (dark purple), this indicates the horse isn't handling the stress well, and the byproducts are causing problems. This can indicate the onset of tying-up or azoturia.

Capillary refill time, tested with a finger pressed to the gum, can indicate the degree of stress present and reflect developing toxemia in the muddy stages. Congestion may progress to cyanosis as the refill time increases to five seconds or more. Normal horses will "pink up" almost as soon as you remove pressure. The scleral vessels of the eyes may also become "injected," turning bloodshot.

Fatigue can sneak up on you if you don't pay attention to what your horse is telling you. Some game horses are perfectly willing to go out and run themselves to death for your benefit, so you have to be aware of their condition.

As fatigue progresses, the horse will become less alert and fail to take interest in his surroundings. He might cease listening to you, begin to set his own pace or slow up. If that's the case, you might be better off to pause for a few minutes to let him graze, rather than trying to continue. While he grazes, check for other fatigue symptoms, such as anal sphincter response, capillary refill, pulse and respiration, dehydration and so forth.

Thumps

Extreme fatigue can result in thumps, otherwise known as synchronous diaphragmatic flutter or exhaustive disease syndrome. It is an involuntary contraction of the diaphragm coordinated with the heart rate, causing the flanks of the horse to twitch and thump.

The diaphragm divides the chest cavity, including lungs and heart, from the abdominal cavity, which contains the stomach and intestines. It is a muscle that assists in breathing and is controlled by the phrenic nerve. It is not absolutely certain what causes the condition, but it may be caused in part by the tip of the heart punching the diaphragm when it is fatigued and sensitive to mechanical stimulation. It may also be associated with low blood potassium and calcium, metabolic alkalosis and dehydration.

Thumps first appear as a twitch or hiccup in the left flank in time with the heart beat. In severe cases, you can hear and see the twitch. If the condition is mild, and the horse shows no other signs of exhaustion, lead him to the next check. Let the horse drink and eat along the trail. If you can hear the thumps, things are serious, and the horse should be allowed to rest while you send for help. He might colic or tie-up in addition to the rest of his problems; if so, walk slowly while waiting for the vet.

The vet will treat it with a potassium and calcium IV if it is severe. In any case, the horse is rested for several hours and watched carefully.

To help prevent thumps, condition the horse well, ride sensibly, be sure he gets enough to drink, and supplement his diet with electrolytes before, during and after rides.

PREVENTIVE MEDICINE: ELECTROLYTES

Electrolytes help maintain body chemical balance and keep nerve impulses flowing properly. They are used up with work and must be redistributed; fatigue begins when the cell can no longer maintain a proper electrolytic balance under the amount of stress present. Waste accumulates, chemical ratios are disrupted, nerve impulses impeded and the cells become less efficient.

You can get electrolytes in a bolus or powder form from your veterinarian, or make your own (see the appendix for Lew's Mix). As we discussed earlier, you should begin adding them to the feed approximately three days before the ride, sprinkling about an ounce over his grain. It hasn't been proven that electrolytes supplied prior to a ride have any special benefit, but it hasn't been disproven, either. It does accustom him to them, and excess electrolytes leave the body through the urine.

Don't fight the horse to get them down his throat. If he is unwilling to eat them in his grain or water, dose him with a pancake syrup or molasses mixture in a clean wormer syringe. The syringe is the best method at a ride, since you know exactly what went in.

You shouldn't give electrolytes constantly between rides. Just before, during, and the day after should be sufficient. An overdose can cause possible problems, and is certainly a waste. And, when using electrolytes, it's even more important that the horse have free access to water.

Dr. Dean Bauman of Corvallis, Oregon suggests that a horse prone to thumps might benefit from extra potassium in his ration. Morton Lite Salt is a low-sodium, high-potassium table salt that can be added to the grain, or used in your electrolyte mix.

Azoturia

Azoturia, also known as tying-up, is a problem that has plagued horse owners for hundreds of years in the form of "Monday Morning Disease." It strikes suddenly, usually in the first part of the ride, and practically paralyzes the horse's hindquarters.

Shortly after you start riding, the horse stiffens up in the hindquarters, with the loin muscles tense and constricted, and a sweat breaks out. Tied-up horses take a sawhorse-like stance and are reluctant to move, in fact, nearly unable. Urination becomes difficult and painful because the horse cannot arch his back and relax. The urine will probably be scant, and may show the severity of the condition by its color.

Urine is normally a straw color, but when azoturia hits, muscle damage occurs, and the breakdown products leave the body in the urine. The products include myoglobin, a red pigment that is involved with oxygen supply. The darker the urine, the more damage has occurred in the muscles, and in the worst cases, the horse may be unable to urinate at all.

Tying-up is most common in stocky, nervous, overweight and poorly conditioned horses. Many are on sweet feed and were rested several days before the ride—without a corresponding reduction in the grain ration. Mares are more susceptible than geldings and stallions, and the problem is more common in cold weather. Once a horse has tied-up, he is prone to a recurrence.

The symptoms come on quickly, during the first part of a workout. The horse shouldn't be moved, and he should be blanketed, or at least have his loins covered, while you seek help. If you move the horse, the problem can spread, increasing the muscle damage. If the case is severe, the horse can be badly disabled, suffer kidney damage, and perhaps die from the effects. Get a veterinarian if the horse "freezes" up badly.

The vet will treat the horse with a relaxant to relieve the muscle spasms. Sometimes that, combined with a little walking, is sufficient to clear the problem up in an hour or so. In worse cases, it is necessary to detoxify the muscles and stabilize the body chemistry with sodium bicarbonate.

Following a mild case, the horse is rested for a few hours, then walked for an hour or so, well-blanketed. He is allowed no grain for three days, but all the hay and water he wants.

Sometimes after a ride, a horse will stiffen up in the hindquarters from exhaustion; this is often called tying-up. It is a case of "the spirit's willing, but the body's not." Did you ever exercise hard, sit down, and find you just couldn't move? That is how your horse feels at this time, and he needs to be walked and loosened up. That's why a pen for free exercise is especially beneficial after a ride.

This stiffness may also appear when the large muscles get a big slosh of cold water, or the horse gets chilled. You should always put a sheet or blanket on the horse after a long ride, unless the weather is very hot. You won't see the sawhorse stance in this situation.

Azoturia occurs after the horse has been working a short period of time. If the horse is reluctant to move his hindlegs after a long day on the trail, it's probably just exhaustion. If you have doubts, ask the veterinarian.

The cause of azoturia is a high-grain ration coupled with a layoff, such as most endurance horses get just before a ride. A hard-working horse is accustomed to burning a lot of carbohydrates, but when he isn't working, they accumulate in his muscles in the form of glycogen. When he goes back to work, the glycogen is broken down faster than the resulting by-products can be removed. The circulation is just not enough to clean up the lactic acid, so the arteries constrict, making the job even tougher. With the inadequate blood supply, the muscles are unable to either relax or contract, and the horse is in a great deal of pain.

Role of Potassium and Calcium. The tying-up syndrome may also be linked to lack of chemical elements like potassium and calcium. Potassium keeps the muscle fibers at their proper level of excitability, and when it's in short supply, the cells contract too readily. Potassium is also responsible for dilation of the blood vessels, improving the circulation and letting the muscles get badly needed oxygen.

Calcium is involved in energy production and is responsible for relaxing muscle fibers after they contract. The scene goes like this: a deficient fiber contracts too quickly, can't get enough oxygen, and can't relax. Artery constriction further limits the oxygen supply, so the muscles switch to anaerobic burning, allowing lactic acid to accumulate.

The exact causes are still debatable, and prevention is the best cure. Reduce your grain ration during layoffs and turn the horse out when he isn't worked. Vitamin E and selenium deficiencies may play a part in tying-up, so be sure that your feed ration includes them.

You can also give injections of E-Se once a week but that can be a nuisance. If you choose to include it in the feed, the horse should have approximately eight milligrams weekly. Be careful not to give the horse too much, as it is cumulative, and too much can lead to toxic effects.

Be sure that the horse's diet is complete in other elements as well. Grain is low in potassium, but alfalfa hay is high in both potassium and calcium. Baking soda (sodium bicarbonate) may be added to the feed if the horse is chronically affected by tying-up, though it's not absolutely proven to be of any benefit. Thiamine (vitamin B_1) may also have some effect.

Colic

Colic is a common complication. The stressed horse may be dehydrated and have minimal blood flow to the digestive system. Too much cold water all at once, a sudden change of feed, or just too much excitement may bring on cramps. The horse will want to roll, and will probably nip or kick at his belly in response to the pain. If he goes down and struggles, the intestinal tract may rupture or twist. Blood clots may interfere with the circulation. If you suspect colic, keep the horse moving, and get the vet immediately.

You can help prevent colic by worming regularly with different classes of wormer, and conditioning thoroughly. Make sure that the horse gets all the water he needs without tanking up too heavily on ice water. The horse needs 10 to 12 gallons of water daily, and even more in high temperatures.

The endurance horse must be in good condition, not overweight, and not too thin. If the problem occurs frequently, perhaps you'd better find another horse, or another sport. Don't feed excessive amounts of grain; increase the energy levels with added oils instead. Carbohydrate loading works fine in the human, but causes azoturia in the equine.

Sometimes a horse goes down with one of these problems, tying-up, thumps, etc., and suffers complications that make it impossible to save him. If he's a little bit wormy, or his worming program was neglected in earlier years, he could be weakened internally, and unable to withstand added stress. Heart disease or congenital weakness might also make it impossible to save the horse. Sometimes these problems would have killed the horse eventually, no matter what he did for a living.

In summary, the exhausted horse may show a number of symptoms, including a high heart rate with pulse irregularities and possibly thumps. The muscles will twitch with fatigue, and the horse will be stiff and reluctant to move. His breathing will be harsh and fail to drop within 30 minutes after coming into a rest stop, remaining inverted for a long period.

Inversion in humid areas means the horse is merely cooling himself the best way he knows, but it is serious if it persists for a long period of time.

The dehydrated horse will have sunken eyes, high temperature, scant urine and possible shock. The mucous membranes will be muddy, and capillary-refill time will be slow. He won't give a darn about eating or going on. No bowel sounds will be present, and the anal sphincter will be totally relaxed.

If the horse shows severe fatigue with many of these symptoms, he's in trouble—and you know darn good and well who did it to him. On the other hand, as a note of etiquette, if you see someone else having problems with their horse, be helpful. Don't kibitz about how stupid he or she was, since you don't know the circumstances involved. It isn't necessary to play judge and jury in these situations.

For successful, trouble-free endurance riding, ride sensibly and take good care of your horse. Chances are, you'll never be faced with a severe problem. However, if a problem appears, the vet is there to help.

After a long ride, your horse is probably going to lie down, flat out, and sleep. Even if he doesn't usually do this, he will now.

When Hanne Hollander finished her first endurance ride, she noticed that the horse was anxious to lie down. Worried, she consulted the veterinarian, fearing that the horse was ill. After a quick look at the horse, he asked her, "Don't you feel like lying down?"

Hanne told him yes.

"Well, so does the horse!"

9: Campaigning the Stallion

A STALLION is a challenge, no matter what the sport. He is not the right mount for a novice horseman, but can put out great efforts for an experienced rider.

Most stallions are campaigned with the aim of promoting them for breeding. It is an expensive form of "advertising" to prove how good the horse is, especially to those breeding endurance stock. The endurance stallion has to have good conformation and be fully sound to compete, plus a good disposition. There are rank stallions on the endurance trail, but they usually don't stay that way for long.

On the other hand, some stallions are so well-mannered that you don't even notice them in a crowd. Tezero, an aged Arabian stallion owned by the Gervais family of Corvallis, Montana, has won many rides and has never been out of the top ten. In 1979, he carried 11-year-old Holly Gervais to the National Junior Championship. Holly learned to ride him at the age of two, and Tezero has done his best for her ever since.

When a stallion comes back to the trails year after year, you know he's got to be good. Surrabu, an Arabian stallion owned by Heidi Smith of Meridian, Idaho, has been on the road eight years so far, and will probably continue competing for years to come.

"MANNERS" ARE IMPORTANT

A stallion can be of flawless conformation and look like an outstanding prospect, but if he hasn't got a good disposition, it's going to be hard to do more than complete rides. If the stallion spends all night neighing at mares, gets fresh at the start and wastes a lot of time in the vet checks recovering, it's going to be a frustrating project, and possibly an entire waste of time. That energy could put you further and faster down the road.

This Arabian stallion, Tezero, has long been a consistent performer on the trail. In 1979, he carried 10-year-old Holly Gervais to the national junior championship, and his daughter, Tezero's Kyzi, tagged along to take the reserve national championship in the senior division for Pat Gervais, Holly's mother.

Good manners start at home. Surrabu lives in a centrally located stallion pen with both mares and geldings nearby, plus a lot of activity next to his pen. Tezero shares his enclosure with mares and colts much of the time. If a horse is constantly isolated from other horses, the excitement of a ride will make him almost uncontrollable, to say nothing of the mental problems that may be developing.

Ideally, a stallion should have a large paddock to run in—two to three acres—and have his own stall. Board fence is safest, and most stallion owners run a hot wire along the top to discourage horses from fighting over the fence. Stallions seem to maintain their condition better because they have more energy and will run around a great deal. They need either a companion or other horses close by.

Heidi points out that a stallion is very territorial and herd conscious. She never puts another horse in Surrabu's paddock when he's not there. She believes that it makes him feel more secure because his territory will be waiting for him to come home to, along with his very own mares.

It is important to develop a definite breeding routine and stick to it so that the horse always knows what he is expected to do. Surrabu only breeds mares in his paddock, so that when he goes out the gate, his mind is on business. Whether it's a special place for breeding, a special halter, or simply an unusual routine, stick to it.

A stud must be disciplined for inappropriate behavior. He shouldn't be picked at constantly, but corrected firmly and promptly when needed.

The Gervais's ride Tezero with mares in heat or other stallions on purpose, teaching him there is a time and a place for everything. Sometimes he will even be ridden with a mare immediately after breeding her. It's all part of building good manners.

Understanding Their Moods

When working with stallions, you must be aware that their moods change a great deal and that emotions play a large role in their behavior. Their high hormone levels can be a help or a hindrance in endurance. There is also a large potential for accidents, both at home and on the road, whereas, as we said before, a mare or gelding might be quieter and more consistent.

It helps to haul a stallion a great deal to training areas so that he doesn't get all worked up about the trip. When training, ride with different people, or alone, trying to anticipate any situations that might occur at a ride. Stallions get bored easily, so try to vary the workouts as much as possible to keep them eager to go.

When hauling a stallion, always load him in the trailer first, before any of the other horses. Let him become accustomed to traveling with mares and geldings alike. When you arrive at your destination, unload the stallion last to prevent any problems with savaging or mounting the other horse. Stay clear of his hindquarters in case he gets excited and tries to kick.

When he's in good shape, it's a good idea for him to have a place to run and play when he's not working. Otherwise that extra energy is taken out on you.

AT THE RIDE

When you go to a ride with a stallion, park on the outskirts of camp where it is quieter. The stallion should always be cross-tied with two lead ropes on the trailer with enough length to allow him to eat comfortably. A well-mannered horse may be no worry, but a rank horse needs the two ropes for insurance.

At the ride the vet check is the biggest worry, since stallions have a higher rate of metabolism. Recovery can be slow sometimes. Checking in can be a riot scene, so you must be alert and make the horse behave.

Watch what he's looking at; it might be a mare in heat. When pulse and respiration are being taken, stand directly in front of the horse's nose, making him watch you instead of the other horses. If he doesn't pay attention to you, use a lead shank with a stud chain as an attention getter. Some studs are just fine with a regular lead rope, but they are big, strong animals, and sometimes you need that extra edge of control.

During the ride itself, many who ride stallions can be seen off hiding in the bushes to get the horse to recover. Otherwise every passing horse sends the pulse rocketing back up with excitement and curiosity.

A stallion has a mind of his own, and most won't stand for being pushed. Instead they sulk and poke along until they are good and ready. Some stallions have poor manners as well, and kick if someone gets too close. Their innate sense of self-preservation discourages them from racing into exhaustion. Natural instincts

Jackie Grape, on the right, rides her purebred Arabian stallion, Arasin, through a ride. Arasin is the first thousand-mile stallion in the Northwest region.

of herd behavior may also have some effect on racing strategy, as a stallion's proper place is at the back of the herd to chivvy up the stragglers. If someone is lagging a mile or two behind you, your stallion may balk and wait for him to catch up.

Surrabu rates himself during a ride, speeding up and slowing down as he pleases. It seems crazy to Heidi, but he places consistently and has had one win so far, doing it all his way!

STALLION TOTEBOARD

Some points to remember in stallion handling include:

Don't continually beat on the horse. You're not big enough to win an all-out fight, so don't provoke one. Instead, psych the horse out and make him respect you. A stallion is stronger than a mare or gelding, and that strength can turn into belligerence, especially with the wrong sort of discipline.

Stallions behave differently, with more tendency to bite, paw and strike, because they are fighters by nature. Don't overhandle them, and don't fool around with their heads more than necessary, because that encourages biting.

Most trainers who handle stallions fear the cuddled backyard pet more than the bronc off the range. The pet usually has no respect, and that's what the entire relationship is built on. In a stall, don't turn your back on him and give him a chance to kick or strike. Let the horse face you first, and preferably come to you for handling. Gentle stallions are no problem in this respect, but every stud is different.

If he bites, a pin will often teach him better manners. Hold the pin so that it pokes him when he turns to nip. Others haul off and slap the muzzle for biting. It all depends on the horse, but the punishment must be swift, sure, and reasonable. Don't club the horse for giving you a dirty look.

The stallion that "talks" all the time can drive you up the wall. It is possible to discipline him and make him be quiet by getting after him each time, either with a swat or a sharp remark. Work on it until he learns to be quiet in normal situations. You can let him be studdy at breeding time, but don't let him get away with it the rest of the time.

Don't lose your temper. That's how you get hurt.

Don't just lightly slap the horse for misbehaving. He'll think that's not any penalty compared to the fun of being bad, and keep testing you.

Be a friend to the horse, but don't get too cuddly. Some horses love it; some will take your arm off.

If you're willing to put up with the special problems of competing with a stallion, you should be able to do well. Stallions are naturally competitive in most cases, especially if it's their own idea.

10: Awards and Achievements

ONE OF THE BASIC premises of endurance riding is that all who finish will receive a completion award. It can be a certificate or a belt buckle, a jacket, or just about anything you can name in the line of horse equipment. Some rides cater to the novice, who likes to take home trophies for his efforts. The more experienced riders often have a mantle full of that stuff already, and prefer taking home a bridle or something that will eventually be of use.

Top-ten riders will receive a fancier completion award, a ribbon, or some little thing to show their placings. The winners of the junior and senior divisions will usually get a trophy or some large award, like a blanket. Some rides give duplicate awards for placings in light- and heavyweight-weight divisions, as well as the junior division.

Breed awards are given to the first registered horse of the most common breeds to finish, plus the first grade horse and the first registered Endurance Horse. Some rides keep these breed awards to a minimum; others recognize every breed entered. Sometimes there are fun awards to recognize oldest and youngest riders, and other oddball choices. It's all part of an effort to make everyone feel recognized.

A few rides offer cash awards, but they are rare. If you want to make money at your hobby, play tennis.

BEST-CONDITION AWARD

Best-condition is the most cherished award, and is given to promote good conditioning and care of the horse. It recognizes the horse that would probably win the next race, if it were held immediately.

The best-condition horse should be capable of another 50 or 100 miles, starting right now.

The most best-condition awards garnered by a single horse in one season is six, and four horses have equalled that record. They are Red, the 1978 national champion, ridden by Tracie Slater; Blanc Seurat, ridden by Jan Worthington; Law Thunder, the 1979 national champion, ridden by Hanne Hollander; and Tezero's Kyzi, the 1979 reserve champion, ridden by Pat Gervais.

Best-condition doesn't always go to the ride winner. There are occasional hard feelings and inconsistencies in selection, and there were changes made at the AERC national convention in 1980 to alleviate those problems.

One of the original problems was in selection of the best-condition candidates. If the first ten horses did not finish close together, they were not stressed equally. If number 1 finished two hours ahead of number 10, he definitely worked harder. Another inequity was in the amount of weight carried. If the winner carried a 60-pound junior, and number 2 was packing 160 pounds, 2 was definitely under more stress.

The new eligibility requirements for best-condition state that all riders, including juniors, light and heavyweights, are eligible for consideration if they were among the first ten horses to finish within 20 percent of the winning time. This means that if the 50-mile ride was won in five hours of riding time, the competitors finishing in the next hour would be eligible for best condition, up to the tenth horse.

Only one best-condition award per ride will be recognized, but the ride management has the option of recognizing best-condition horses in different divisions, including a runner-up or top three, if he so chooses. If there are no acceptable horses as candidates, the award need not be given.

The AERC point system no longer gives bonus points for winning best-condition, but will recognize the horse and rider team that won the most best-condition awards during the season.

The Point System

The ride veterinarians are in charge of selecting the best-conditioned horse, using a special score sheet and point system. At least two vets will look the horses over within an hour after the last eligible horse finishes, probably during the one hour recheck. Up to 100 points can be given for good physical condition following the ride. No lame horses will be considered, unless they are just slightly off, with no definite sore leg or legs.

The items evaluated on the veterinary score sheet include pulse and respiration, hydration, mucous membranes, capillary-refill, gut sounds, muscle soreness and back pain, way of going, filling or swelling of the joints, tendons and ligaments, sores and galls, if any, and attitude, willingness and coordination. The horse is disqualified if he is severely dehydrated, failed to recover to established pulse and respiration criteria, was colicky or lame, tied-up, or severely injured.

The second category is riding time, with the ride winner getting an automatic 100 points for having the fastest time. Each contender will have a point deducted for every minute he or she was behind the winning horse. For example, with a five-hour winning time on a 50-miler, the first place horse would get his 100 points, and the rider who finished an hour later would get 40 points. The horse who came in 20 minutes after the winner would get 80 points.

The third category is rider weight, with all the eligible riders being weighed in their riding clothes, exclusive of tack, immediately after crossing the finish line. The heaviest of those riders would get 100 points, and the other riders would be docked a point per pound. If the heaviest rider was 175 pounds, he would get the 100 points. If the lightest rider weighed 125 pounds, he would get 50 points. A 150-pound rider would get 75 points in this category. If any rider weighed 75 pounds, he'd get no points at all in this category, since they would all be subtracted.

In theory, the winning horse with the heaviest rider that scored the most points on the veterinary criteria would win best-condition for accumulating the most points in all categories. However, there are many possible combinations.

MILEAGE POINTS

The award that every finisher gets is mileage points, and AERC keeps score on every participant in endurance rides. Point awards are given to honor achievements, and encourage more frequent participation.

Along with mileage points, you can get points for a top-ten placing and winning a ride. Bonus points for winning come to half a point per mile, meaning that you would get 25 extra points for winning a 50-miler. You get a point per mile plus a percentage of the mileage points for making the top-ten, with the winner getting full mileage points plus a bonus for winning. Number 2 gets mileage points plus a 90 percent bonus, and so forth.

Rides with less than 10 starters would only give bonus top-ten points in relation to the number of starters. If five started the race, there would only be 50 percent of the top-ten bonus points awarded, with the other points awarded as usual.

That means winning a 50-mile ride would give you 50 mileage points, 50 points for being first in the top ten, and a 25-point bonus for winning. Points add up very quickly!

Senior division riders must be at least 16 years old on January 1 of the year of competition, and may fall into either the light or heavyweight category, depending on whether they weigh more or less than 160. The weight divisions often turn into a men's and women's division, with a few exceptions.

The juniors have their own division and points.

Point awards are given to the top 25 horse and rider teams nationally, and to the top ten regionally. Area groups will also have their own award systems.

There is a mileage program for riders that records only mileage ridden, regardless of placing. Chevrons are awarded as a rider completes the mileage requirements, from 250 upward to 500, and so forth. At this time, lifetime mileage records are crawling into the 5,000s and 6,000s—and that's a lot of miles to ride. The national top-ten seniors and national top-ten juniors are recognized with special awards.

HORSE AWARDS

The 1,000-mile-horse awards recognize the horses that have completed 1,000 competitive miles, and encourage riders to take good care of their horses for a longer riding life. Many horses are at their best after finishing 1,000 miles. Horses are also recognized at the 2,000- and 3,000-mile marks. It shouldn't be long before some make the 4,000-mile total.

Some riders take years to accumulate those big mileage totals, but Robert Manley rode his Morgan, Caballero, over 1,700 miles in 26 rides, and in a single season. That was an all-time record in 1979.

AERC also has a Hall of Fame to recognize special individuals

All eight of these horses are veterans of at least 1,000 miles on the endurance trail for the Hollander family. They've all proven to have what it takes.

and horses for their contributions to endurance riding. A newer award is given for the stallion who covers the most miles in a season. The Jim Jones Award is in memory of a devoted endurance rider, now deceased, who campaigned an Arabian stallion, Rowel.

There is also a 100-mile horse and rider award, using the regular point system, but counting only 100-mile rides. The same horse must be used. This award is to encourage riders to participate in more 100-milers, and the top five nationally are recognized.

Points are also kept for family and husband/wife teams, with the top five getting special awards. That's another reason to make it a family sport!

Regional associations give awards for their members that are similar to the AERC awards in format, recognizing the top riders, both in points and mileage. Breed groups also give awards on a national and local basis, and more are encouraging endurance riding all the time.

BREED AWARDS

The Appaloosa Horse Club offers a number of awards to dedicated riders and their horses, and pioneered an outstanding medallion program to encourage versatility in the breed. The top award is the distance medallion, earned with 300 miles in a single calendar year, in either endurance or competitive trail rides.

The medallion awards are progressive, and given for excellence in racing, endurance, halter and performance. The first award won by the horse, in any category, is bronze; a second medallion in another category is silver. Gold is the third award, and only a few horses have earned a gold medallion. The ultimate medallion is the diamond. No one has yet received that one, as it means an outstanding horse, capable of racing on the flat and on the trail, doing top performance work and looking like a model at halter. Those horses do exist, and the Appaloosa Horse Club is encouraging their development.

The Appaloosa Horse Club also offers a 1,000-mile award for endurance horses, with no time limit, and the top Appaloosa in the nation is recognized annually.

Saddle Log awards are for the rider, given on the basis of time spent riding, on any number of horses and in any sport. The total hour awards go as high as 2,500 hours.

A distance riding patch is given for the first 100 hours of riding time, or the first completed endurance ride, with an additional chevron for each ride after that. The Chief Joseph Commemorative Award goes to the riders who complete 1,000 saddle-log hours, 10 competitive trail rides and 10 endurance rides. It is also a rider award, and any number of horses may be used.

The International Arabian Horse Club (IAHA) has an achievement award program, based on the former Legion of Merit award. There are three levels of recognition, with a Legion of Honor, Legion of Merit and Legion of Supreme Merit. You can earn points by completing an endurance ride, and by placing first through fourth. A distance-award program for endurance horses, similar to the one offered for competitive trail horses, is in the works.

The American Morgan Horse Association recently instituted an endurance award, including a championship and reserve championship plaque, with cash awards of $100 to the champion and $50 to the reserve horse. The AERC point system is used to determine the champions. A Morgan Medallion Award is also offered, requiring the completion of 500 miles that can be earned in either competitive or endurance rides. A medallion is given for each 500 miles completed.

The Tennessee Walking Horse Breeders' and Exhibitors' Association offers an incentive award of $500 to the first Tennessee Walking Horse to rank in the national AERC top-ten. As of 1979, the award was still available. If you are interested in trying for this award, write to the association for current information.

Other breed associations that recognize endurance horses are the Pinto Horse Association of America, the Galiceno Horse Breeders

Association, the Missouri Fox Trotter and the American Indian Horse (total hours on horseback only). The American Donkey and Mule Society also takes an interest in the long-eared clan.

If you want your breed association to recognize endurance horses, write to them and inform them about your participation. Tell them how many of their breed compete, and let them know that you would like recognition. These awards are worked for, not just invented out of thin air. Sponsorship may be required to get them off the ground.

You can get information about any of these programs by writing to the associations involved. Changes are made from year to year, so you should request current requirements.

ENDURANCE RECORDS

From year to year, records are broken in endurance riding. Overall participation is increasing, and more is learned all the time about getting more and more out of the horse without harm.

It is difficult to compare speed records from different rides, as the terrain and climate differ. To be completely fair, you can only compare times for the same ride. Rules also differ, and that can make a difference in speed.

Louise Riedel rode Caprison through a 50-mile ride in 2:29 in 1977, and Lon Seneker took Mountain Storm the same distance in 2:24 in 1978. In 1979, Rushcreek Ernie, ridden by Shirley Gregory completed 50 miles in 2:35. That's fast riding, but very risky for the horse.

In the 100-mile division, James Coffman took Revel D through in 8:09 in 1974. Elwin Wines rode Miss Fit 100 miles in 8:15 in 1975 at the Oregon 100. Hanne Hollander rode Law Thunder over the same course in 1978 in 8:23. Winkie Mackay-Smith took her horse, Silver, through 100 miles in 8:25.

Lew Hollander currently holds the record for 150 miles with 19:35, and Hanne Hollander covered 200 miles in 30:24 in 1979.

Winning times normally range from 3½ hours up for 50-mile rides, to 10 hours or more for 100 miles. However, just because a ride has a lengthy finishing time, it doesn't indicate that everyone rode slowly. Sometimes it's absolutely impossible to go any faster.

The most wins in one year to date was 12, by Red, the 1978 national champion, closely followed by 11 for Blaze, the 1977 champion, ridden by Dayton Osborn. The most best-conditions won by any horse in one year is six, as mentioned earlier.

The most-miles-in-a-year record is held by Caballero, with 1,700 miles. A mule, Deacon, ridden by Mark Erickson, had 1,200 miles for the top place in 1977, but that record was beaten by several in 1979.

Records, of course, are made to be broken, and most of these probably won't stand many years. Maybe you'd like to try to knock one down.

11: The Endurance Horse Registry of America

THE ENDURANCE HORSE REGISTRY of America was founded in 1974 for the preservation, development and improvement of the equine athlete.

It is the only registry where papers are earned solely on the basis of performance. To be eligible for registration as an Endurance Horse, a horse must complete at least 300 miles in one year or make the top-ten twice in races of at least 50 miles with at least 50 contestants. If there are fewer entrants, then horses finishing in the top 10 percent will qualify.

Foals born to two registered Endurance Horses are automatically registered, but cannot produce registered offspring until they themselves have qualified with mileage or placings.

PRIME PURPOSE OF EHRA

Recognizing outstanding equine athletes is the prime purpose of the EHRA, regardless of their breed or type. All must be sound with plenty of stamina. Even geldings are registered, for though they aren't much use in a breeding program, it shows accomplishment and will benefit their breeder by achievements. A colt from a mare who has already produced one or more EHRA qualifiers will be a better prospect for endurance racing, or any other athletic event.

Eventually the EHRA hopes to develop a breed of Endurance Horses from the information gathered on bloodlines and type. Career records are also important in developing a breeding program.

The first registered Endurance Horse was Crickett, owned by Diane Ripley, in 1974. In 1976, Crickett had the first registered

154

The Endurance Horse Registry of America is one of the few registries in the world with a performance requirement, and probably the only American registry where papers are earned solely for achievement.

Endurance Horse foal, Shawnee, sired by Hooshan, an EHRA-registered Arabian stallion.

Jackie Grape of Cove, Oregon has a registered mother and daughter pair, both with over 1,000 miles of competition. They are Tennessee Walkers. The dam is Allen's Golden Queen, also known as Snowball, and the daughter is Allen's Golden Miss, or Missy.

Jackie Grape (number 48) escorts Marion Wood through the Prineville Ride on Allen's Golden Miss (Missy), while riding Allen's Golden Queen (Snowball). They are mother and daughter, and both have over a thousand miles. Jackie hopes eventually to develop a breeding program of EHRA-registered mares, using her thousand-mile stallion, Arasin.

EHRA keeps records for national and regional championships, sponsors an invitational championship ride, and offers a calendar of ride information with pictures of outstanding horses.

There is a Legion of Merit award for horses that reach the 1,500-mile mark in their careers, and a Hall of Fame to recognize the greatest horses. Hall of Fame members must complete 2,500 miles of competition.

All recognized endurance rides will offer a silver cup, sponsored by the EHRA, to the first registered Endurance Horse crossing the finish line. Many top horses are building quite a collection.

EHRA RIDE RULES

In order for a ride to be approved by the EHRA, it must be open to all breeds and not limited to novice competitors, and there must be completion awards available to all finishers.

The ride must be at least 50 miles long and run as a race, with the first horse to cross the line winning.

If the starts are staggered, then the horse finishing in the least amount of elapsed time is the winner. There must be a maximum-time allowance for completion, but no minimum time designated.

For the safety of the horses, the veterinarians must have control of the ride, separate from the ride management.

In rides that use weight divisions, the rules apply for each division.

It takes a good horse to go the distance, and the Endurance Horse Registry will make sure they are recognized for their achievements.

12: And the Horse Makes Three

WHAT SPORT is one-third marathon, one-third horse race and one-third crazy? It's "Ride-and-Tie," which originated as a way to get the most out of one horse when two people needed it.

The practice of Ride-and-Tie goes far back into history, but the Levi Strauss Corporation of San Francisco is responsible for promoting the rebirth of it. Modern Ride-and-Tie was the brainchild of Bud Johns, a publicity director for the well-known blue jeans makers. He had read about it in some newspaper clippings dating back about a hundred years ago and thought it would make a neat race. After he went to work for Levi Strauss, he presented the thought to them as a promotion—and ever since, Ride-and-Tie races have flourished.

The Levi's Ride-and-Tie is the biggest and best race of all, and is held in different locations each year, with distances varying. In 1979, 118 teams started the 36-mile race at Sunriver, Oregon.

RIDE-AND-TIE RULES

The rules are simple—the mavericks who enter like it that way. A team consists of two runners and one horse. Only one person may use the horse for forward progress at a time—in other words; one can't be aboard and the other tailing at the same time. The horseman rides ahead a reasonable distance and ties the horse. He (or she) bails off and runs on, while the runner comes up to get the horse. When they catch the first runner, they go on a bit further, tie the horse and trade off. You can tie as often as you like, as long as you change a minimum number of times, until

157

crossing the line. Your time is determined by the last team member to cross the line.

It seems like a formidable sport, but it is really fast and easy to cover long distances in this leap-frog manner. When you are exhausted, hopefully the horse will be near. You get a bit of rest while passing your partner. Excitement helps carry you through until the finish line appears and you find that you really have run quite a distance.

There is a book, *Ride and Tie, The Challenge of Running and Riding,* by Don Jacobs, that covers the subject very thoroughly. Rather than duplicate his work, this chapter will present some basic hints and ideas on getting started.

THE RIGHT HORSE

There are some differences in selecting a Ride-and-Tie horse. He must be small, making it easy to mount and dismount quickly. An older, mature horse, at least 10 years old, will stay sounder and handle the stress much better because of his experience.

During Ride-and-Tie racing, the horse sprints for a mile or a mile and a half, then stands and waits for the runner. That's hard on his body, and that's why an experienced horse is needed. He has to have a history of complete soundness because the veterinarians along the way will be very particular.

A Ride-and-Tie horse must have excellent recovery rates since the stops are all stop and go. It can be frustrating to come into a stop and find that your partner has gone on, but that the horse is still not down and ready to leave.

A large heart and lungs will make it easier for him to recover from the stress, and experience will have taught him to relax promptly. After all, there might be another 50 horses racing past while he stands tied to a tree. Some horses will go nuts, and either break loose or hang themselves [literally] before the runner arrives.

The horse has to be capable of covering ground without a lot of riding, allowing a worn out runner to take a breather. The rider won't be helping the horse much, so he'll have to do it pretty much on his own. A reliable horse with a comfortable gait will make it possible for the rider to recover.

One of the biggest problems is spotting your horse out of dozens of look-alikes. A uniquely colored or marked horse will make it less likely that you'll run past him. Running past your own horse? Come on! Yet, it's surprisingly common. In the past, both human team members have crossed the finish line, only to realize that the horse was out in the brush somewhere, tied to a tree and waiting for rescue. That meant one runner had to trek back out and find him—perhaps a run of 10 miles or more.

At the 1979 Levi race, one team tried to solve that problem with a transistor radio. Dean Hubbard knew that his partner, Hans Minet, had a tendency to run past the horse. The idea was that the radio would be turned on every time the horse was tied. Somewhere along the line, Dean forgot, and Hans missed the horse. The mistake was quickly remedied, and the horse came across the line to music.

A fluorescent orange collar, ribbons on the saddle, you'll see dozens of different ways to make the horse highly visible. Someday there'll probably be a zebra out there.

The horse must be very fast, a sprinter as opposed to the distance Arabian, and capable of sprinting a mile or so. He'll get a breather while the runner catches up. The distance horse may be too slow for Ride-and-Tie competition.

RIDE-AND-TIE STRATEGY

In Ride-and-Tie, the horse is expendable, and the runners are to be preserved. That's exactly the opposite from endurance, where the horse is the key to winning strategy. As long as the horse clears the vet stops, there is no rating, just flat out going.

This philosophy varies, according to the team runners. Two world-class marathoners might feel the horse was the weak one of the team, and would run with him to save his energy.

It isn't necessary to be a world marathoner, though, to win Ride-and-Tie races. The teams vary, from two men, two women, to mixed pairs. People of all ages are out there, from kids to mature folk.

During the race, the horse should make it to the vet stops ahead of runner number 2. That way runner number 1 can go ahead, letting the horse recover. If some goof makes it the other way around, the whole team is set back.

The runners should know the trail in advance. They should plan ahead where to tie the horse, and decide which spot will be the final tie before going into the vet check.

The plan should call for the horse to spend three to eight minutes in the stop, and to be ready to continue when the next runner arrives.

As in endurance riding, a crew can be very helpful. Only a competitor can take the horse to be vetted, but anyone can assist at a vet stop. The crew, for instance, can take care of the horse while the rider runs on ahead. On the trail, however, the runners are on their own.

The number of vet stops will vary according to ride length, and the horse must meet strict criteria all the way, as well as passing a check after the race's end.

The Correct "Tie"

Some "tricks of the trade" can save a lot of time on the trail. The tie is extremely important; a rope with a snap on each end is used. The halter must be stout and well fitted, for the horse might fight being tied.

The two-snap rope makes it possible just to snap the rope around a convenient tree. An actual knot is prone to jamming and can

Only a competitor can take the horse for the vet examinations during the race itself. The horse must be experienced enough to recover quickly and handle the stress of short, hard runs and rest breaks.

Lew demonstrates his tie rope with the snap on both ends for convenience in tying on the trail. Not having to fool with a knot can save valuable seconds in a close race.

Al Paulo demonstrates his Pony Express-style mount for Ride-and-Tie races. It only takes a few seconds to get underway—and seconds win races, not minutes. Be forewarned that if you don't make it on in the first jump, the horse can take off and make you run very fast to keep up.

be hard to handle when you're tired. A weary runner will find a simple, large snap easier to manage.

It should only take three to four seconds to bail off and tie the horse, using a snap rope. Seconds count because the riders are on and off so much. Al Paulo, Lew Hollander's partner, can vault on the horse, which saves time. Those who run better than they ride often waste time when trying to mount an excited horse. Vaulting saves a lot of fighting because the horse is already loose and on the go. Al can be on the way in three or four seconds, compared to 10 or 12 for the usual change.

If a team saves five seconds or more per change, and makes 20 changes, it could make up a minute or two throughout the ride, and that could mean a better placing at the end.

When tying the horse, it shouldn't be where the trail is steep.

Even if the tree looks inviting, it won't work unless the horse can circle the tree and move around. Otherwise, he could fall or injure himself.

A stout tree that won't bend or break is what's wanted. If the first tree chosen proves inadequate for the task, the rider should go on and find a better one. The best area is one that lets his partner see the horse as long as possible. The runner will be slow to react, and should be given every opportunity to realize _this is the horse_.

Two major things can go wrong in Ride-and-Tie racing. The horse can be pulled or delayed at a check, and the runner can run past the horse. Both are utterly frustrating after all that work!

Ride-and-Tie can teach you what your horse is going through because you're running right through the dust with him. You learn to appreciate just how good he is when you encounter problems. You also learn about real teamwork.

RIDE-AND-TIE RACES

In the past, Ride-and-Tie races have been relatively short. They are getting longer though, with at least one 50-miler on the schedule. Eventually, the races may be 100 miles or more. At the longer distances, the horse will definitely become the weak member of the team, since a human recovers faster than a horse. The longer rides will also give experienced endurance riders an advantage, since they will have a better understanding of their horses. Without a horse, the team goes nowhere.

When you are ready for an even bigger challenge, there are several endurance rides that allow runners to compete over the same course. The Old Dominion Ride and the Tevis, both 100-milers, allow runners a crack at finishing the distance inside of the 24-hour limit. It can be done, but it's tough.

The idea got started when Californian Gordy Ainsleigh had his horse go lame the week before the Tevis. He decided to run it instead, and covered the route in 23:42. This pioneer effort led to others trying it, to get a most appropriate buckle, made especially for Tevis runners. Similar to the Tevis buckle, it has a figure of Hermes instead of the pony express rider. Hermes was the Greek messenger of the gods, if you recall, and the conductor of the dead to Hades. How appropriate!

13: The Versatile Athlete

THE HORSE is an extremely versatile animal, capable of jumping a seven-foot wall, or sliding to a stop at high speed. An individual horse is capable of learning many maneuvers, but few are really good at many different events because the skills are so different.

The stocky cow horse capable of flipping a steer end over end in the arena won't be a standout in the working-hunter division. He can probably jump, but he won't look graceful at it. On the other hand, he'll probably do an excellent job at calf-roping and bull-dogging because the same skills are used.

SKILLS OF THE ENDURANCE HORSE

Let's look at the skills an endurance horse uses. He has to cover a lot of ground in a minimum of time, traveling efficiently and smoothly. He has to jump banks, logs and such in rugged terrain, taking it all calmly and quietly. A clumsy horse will soon injure himself, or scare his rider, so he doesn't last long at endurance.

The endurance horse has to maintain his balance on precarious trails, collecting himself to climb and descend hills. He can remain strung out on slopes, but it isn't an effective way to use himself. He also learns to go over whatever's in front of him, whether it's a boulder patch or a bog. He learns to settle down and get to work. After a few hundred miles, runaways learn to save a little something for the long haul.

Good Show Training

Those are all useful skills in the horse world. A goofy or sour show horse will relax and pay attention to his rider after a few long rides, instead of watching for dinosaurs in the bushes.

Endurance riding is a good cure for sourness in show horses,

165

with a few fringe benefits. Trail riding provides both variety and body-building in training. The excellent conditioning will make it possible for him to perform at a high standard throughout a long class, and a long show. It might take five miles of galloping to work him down before breakfast, but he'll show all day and half the night before he wears out.

Lack of impulsion is a big problem in any horse, dressage or show, that gets a lot of ring work. Continual circling of a small area does not encourage a long, reaching stride. Some horses are physically weak or bad-mannered, both of which can show up as a hollow back with the head above the bit. The gaits will drag and get sloppy, as shown in the four-beat canter. Conditioning isn't a guaranteed cure for problems like those, but it can really help.

A well-conditioned horse and rider will ride more aggressively

Cross-country work teaches a horse to move freely with a good length of stride. The extension at the trot in this picture, taken on a slight downhill slope, is characteristic of a first-level dressage horse. As the carrying capacity of the hindquarters increases, the horse will be able to lengthen even more.

in competition. Those long hours spent together will pay off in better performance and rapport. A weak seat and legs will improve a thousand percent after a few hundred miles in the two-point position. It's a great way to build up confidence in your riding, and showing won't be nearly so intimidating afterward.

A rank horse improves a great deal with a lot of trail riding, learning to accept the rider and his guidance instead of searching for evasions. There are a lot of screwy horses that have never been tired in their lives—and it shows. They get worked half an hour, bathed, and stabled. Those long, lazy hours give them a lot of time to think about getting out of what little work they get.

Hard work will improve a horse physically as well as mentally. Short strides will lengthen, and long strides will become smoother and steadier. Performance will be more consistent because the horse won't tire as quickly, and he'll learn faster with a better attention span.

A year on the endurance trail will really develop the muscling of the average horse, with the gaskins and forearms really increasing in diameter. The body functions become more efficient. Bones increase slightly in diameter, in response to the stress, while the tendons and ligaments thicken and strengthen, meaning less chance of injury.

The masters of horsemanship have long acknowledged the benefits of cross-country work in developing all-around horses that were a pleasure to ride.

In Waldemar Seunig's book, *Horsemanship,* he comments that a lack of gymnastic training (dressage and jumping) causes a horse's legs to wear out prematurely because an inflexible back does not take up the concussion. An elastic back is derived from a balance of cross-country and ring work.

Seunig also says that a horse that doesn't move forward in a correct posture, stressing muscles unevenly, will take short strides and move more slowly than a well-trained horse, even if his conformation is better than that of the trained horse. The unschooled horse takes shorter steps that are less springy, increasing the chance of injury and wearing out both the horse and rider much sooner than necessary.

Seunig goes on to say that the average horse overloads his forehand, seeking his balance in the reins and wasting energy. It's easier to carry a balanced load, but if the horse isn't taught to travel in horizontal balance with an equal part of his weight on the forehand and hindquarters, he must learn it for himself. This can be a slow process, but eventually he learns to collect himself naturally.

Alois Podhajsky, former head of the Spanish Riding School and noted dressage trainer, comments in his book, *Riding Teacher,* that cross-country work strengthens and straightens the horse. Impulsion and vigor are restored, and the horse learns to relax.

Podhajsky also comments that a dressage horse or jumper that can't be ridden outdoors, due to temperament or other problems, shows a deficiency in his schooling. He took every possible opportunity to work his dressage horses and the Lippizaners cross-country. The same holds true for Hilda Gurney today, who takes her dressage horse, Keen, out trail riding regularly.

You must use discretion, though. Taking an expensive horse out hacking presents little risk, but there is always a possibility of injury in the rugged sport of endurance riding. A stumble can mean the end of years of training. Usually, a horse trained to third-level dressage, or above, is not risked in other events. He's proven himself excellent at his specialty. At this point, trail riding is just a change of pace, keeping him relaxed and refreshed.

Eventing and Endurance

The sport of three-day eventing, with dressage, cross-country and stadium jumping, is probably best suited to most endurance horses. The athletic skills of the endurance horse would serve him well on the courses. In fact, there are endurance trails that are tougher than pre-training level horse trials.

If this interests you, you should probably pick a horse taller than the average trail horse, paying a little more attention to his fine conformation points and way of going.

Just think, a horse accustomed to going 50 miles would find it childishly simple to cover the short roads and tracks asked for in lower levels. The obstacles wouldn't be as formidable as those at low levels, either, not like those at Ledyard or Burghley.

At the pre-training or novice level, you would be expected to perform a simple training-level dressage test, asking for large circles and the working gaits. The cross-country and stadium fences wouldn't be over three feet in height, or more than three feet, three inches wide. The cross-country would only be about a mile and a half long, with 12 to 15 obstacles.

Eventing is risky, with a lot of injuries, but most of them happen to tired horses that lose their resilience. He fails to clear a rail, or makes a clumsy approach, or pecks on landing. The endurance horse will stay fresher longer, and have the advantage of stronger tendons and muscles. He'll know how to use himself better, and probably buck you off at the end of the course.

If you are interested in combined training, you should take lessons in dressage and jumping from a good instructor. You'll ride more confidently, get more out of your horse, and have more fun.

Some endurance horses are used exclusively on the trails, but most people have one or two horses that do everything. That can be an advantage, because the horse stays fresh longer. Endurance horses get bored and sour, too.

Gaming can liven up a stale horse. The distance work will probably take the edge off his speed, but the athletic ability and conditioning will make up for it. A soft horse can't go flat out through an entire game course without running out of steam, but with proper training a tough endurance mount will do his best all the way.

Horse showing is another change of pace, but you have to choose your classes carefully, considering your horse's type, and degree of training. For some reason, trail class judges are not impressed when you zip through their course in 33 seconds flat. Western pleasure can also be a weak event, but the English division can be perfect for a good horse.

It would also be interesting to see how endurance-trained horses do at flat racing. There have been one or two endurance horse races on the track, but they were only competing against themselves, not racers. It's unlikely, though, that there will ever be races carded that allow aged, unraced maidens to compete.

Don't limit yourself and your horse to a single activity. Horses are too interesting, and too diverse. It's impossible to condition all of the time.

An ideal training program will alternate distance work with advanced schooling, allowing you to develop a dressage or show horse in the peak of condition. That's called building an athlete. You provide the options, and you can create one heck of a horse.

If you're saying, "Why would anyone want a well-trained horse out in the woods, anyway?" There are a lot of half-broken horses out there, but it helps to have power steering instead of four-fisted drive. Surely you've seen someone trying to winch a runaway horse around a hairpin turn. On the other hand, a trained horse will do a rollback and be on his way, long before the other horse even figures out where the trail went.

Another scenario finds you trotting along a crooked, wooded trail. Suddenly you spot a stump, aimed directly at your knee, but it's too late to rein around it. Instinctively, you apply your leg and bend the horse's body around the stump, saving your knee for future use. That's where all that suppling and bending pays off.

Maybe you're running with a large group of horses and see a cattle guard ahead. You can turn for the gate, if no one else is in your way, and if your horse is responsive enough. You can stop, letting everyone else plow into you, probably knocking you into the middle of it. Or you can lean forward, squeeze with your legs and drive the horse into a leap. Jumping a cattle guard is a poor idea, but it sure beats running across one.

Jumping skills give you a lot more options on difficult trails, and you'll know more about your horse's capabilities. I've noticed that the horse who knows how to jump will use his hindquarters more effectively in climbing embankments, and evade hazards more easily.

So do other things with your endurance horse. He'll enjoy the variety, and someday the skills might pay off.

Endurance riding is a solitary sport most of the time. You condition alone because most of your friends can't keep up with you; you ride alone in the endurance rides a lot of the time. It's just your horse and you, taking on a big challenge. Good luck!

A: Addresses of Trail Organizations and Breed Associations that Promote Endurance Riding

TRAIL ORGANIZATIONS

AMERICAN ENDURANCE RIDE CONFERENCE
P.O. Box 1
Auburn, CA 95603

AUSTRALIAN ENDURANCE RIDE ASSOCIATION
Patsie Sinfield
Wilstenholme Avenue
Bringelly, 2171
Australia

CALIFORNIA STATE HORSEMAN'S ASSOCIATION
P.O. Box 1179
Santa Rosa, CA 95402

EASTERN STATES TRAIL RIDE ASSOCIATION
P.O. Box 142
Douglasville, GA 30133

HAWAII ENDURANCE AND TRAIL RIDERS ASSOCIATION
P.O. Box 451
Kailua-Kona, HI 96740

MOUNTAIN REGION ENDURANCE RIDERS
9002 No. Highway 85
Littleton, CO 80125

NATIONAL COMMITTEE OF FRANCE ENDURANCE RIDERS
Pierre Passemard
Combelcau-Flaugnac
46170 Castelnau-Montratier
France

NATIONAL TRAILS COUNCIL
P.O. Box 1042
St. Charles, IL 60174

NEBRASKA ENDURANCE AND COMPETITIVE TRAIL RIDE
ASSOCIATION
P.O. Box 83047
Lincoln, NE 68501

NORTH ALABAMA ENDURANCE AND TRAIL RIDERS
ASSOCIATION
Rt. 1, Box 100
Madison, AL 35758

PACIFIC NORTHWEST ENDURANCE RIDERS
Rt. 1, Box 80
Powell Butte, OR 97753

ROCKY MOUNTAIN CONFERENCE
2011 Williams
Helena, MT 59601

SOUTHWEST ENDURANCE RIDERS
12798 9th St.
Yucaipa, CA 92399

TRAIL RIDING ALBERTA CONFERENCE
Karen Armstrong
RR1
Rocky Mountain House
Alberta, Canada TOM 1TO

TRAIL BLAZER
P.O. Box 1855
Paso Robles, CA 93446

TRAILS UNLIMITED
Sharon Saare
5722 Keystone Place N.
Seattle, WA 98103

UPPER MIDWEST ENDURANCE AND COMPETITIVE RIDES
ASSOCIATION
455 Moore Heights
Dubuque, IA 52001

Breed Associations

AMERICAN BASHKIR CURLY REGISTRY
P.O. Box 453
Ely, NV 89301

AMERICAN DONKEY AND MULE SOCIETY
Rt. 5, Box 65
Denton, TX 76201

AMERICAN INDIAN HORSE REGISTRY
Rt. 1, Box 64
Lockhart, TX 78644

AMERICAN MORGAN HORSE ASSOCIATION, INC.
Box 1
Westmoreland, NY 13490

APPALOOSA HORSE CLUB
P.O. Box 8403
Moscow, ID 83843

ENDURANCE HORSE REGISTRY OF AMERICA
P.O. Box 63
Agoura, CA 91301

GALICENO HORSE BREEDERS ASSOCIATION
111 East Elm St.
Tyler, TX 75702

INTERNATIONAL ARABIAN HORSE ASSOCIATION
P.O. Box 4502
Burbank, CA 91053

MISSOURI FOX TROTTING HORSE BREED ASSOCIATION
P.O. Box 637
Ava, MO 65608

THE PINTO HORSE ASSOCIATION OF AMERICA, INC.
7525 Mission Gorge Road, Suite C
San Diego, CA 92120

TENNESSEE WALKING HORSE BREEDERS' AND EXHIBITORS'
ASSOCIATION
P.O. Box 286
Lewisburg, TN 37091

B: ELECTROLYTES

LEW'S MIX

IN RESPONSE to the high cost of electrolytes, Lew Hollander developed his own formulation, made from readily available household ingredients at small expense. He is not a veterinarian, but a physicist, and designed his mixture to correspond with typical commercial electrolyte formulas.

Lew's Mix costs about 2¢ per dose, compared to 50¢ or more for a dose of commercial electrolytes. It does not contain excess glucose or sugar bases that tend to make the supplement distasteful to a horse. Most electrolytes available from a veterinarian are designed for sick livestock and intravenous administration, not feeding on a regular basis.

The recipe is as follows:

16 ounces (1 lb.) table salt	$ .29
22 ounces Morton Lite Salt (two boxes)	.70
1 ounce magnesium salts	.06 (approx.)
	$1.05

For the magnesium salts, you may add magnesium carbonate, oxide or sulfate, in the form of Epsom Salts. Carbonate may be preferable, as oxide is slightly less soluble, and sulphate is a cathartic. However, the amount is so small, it isn't likely to have adverse effects.

The table salt raises the sodium concentration. This is necessary because Lite Salt alone is too high in potassium, which can interfere with the magnesium absorption. You need a balance of sodium, potassium and magnesium ions.

Table 4
LEW'S MIX AND OTHER ELECTROLYTE SUPPLEMENTS

	Lew's Mix	Morton Lite Salt	Jug Equi-Ade Prod	Polysal Cutter Lab	Medi Lyte Med Tech	Extralyte Diamond Lab
Sugar	None	0.04%	87.4%	None	79.76%	None*
Sodium Chloride	66.7%	45.52%	8.3%	31.18%	9.68%	32.8%
Potassium Chloride	30.00%	53.69%	3.0%	12.62%	1.27%	43.7%
Magnesium Salts	2.5%	0.25%	0.5%	0.7%	.65%	3.3%
Calcium Salts	None	0.5%	0.8%	5.4%	1.28%	20.1%
Sodium Citrate	None	None	None	None	7.36%	None
Suggested Dosage	1 oz.	—	8¼ oz.	2 oz.	2 oz.	—
	38.8	—	235 gr.	77.6 gr.	77.6 gr.	—
	grams					
Amount of Sodium	18.9 gr.	13 gr.	19.5 gr.	24 gr.	7.5 gr.	9.3 gr.
Amount of Potassium	8.5 gr.	15.3 gr.	7 gr.	9.8 gr.	1.0 gr.	12.5 gr.
Amount of Magnesium	0.71 gr.	0.07 gr.	1.2 gr.	0.5 gr.	0.5 gr.	0.5 gr.

* These values are only estimates.

NOTE: Information is based on label data and inquiries with the companies.

The mix is given in the feed prior to the ride, and in a wormer syringe during the ride. One ounce of electrolyte mix is combined with about two ounces of pancake syrup (unbuttered) for use. Pancake syrup is used instead of molasses, because it will flow at any temperature and lasts forever.

The table gives a breakdown of Lew's Mix and other popular supplements.

C: American Endurance Ride Conference Best Condition Evaluation Scoresheet

American Endurance Ride Conference

Administrative Offices:
Route 5, Box 79DA, Stilson Canyon Rd., Chico, California 95926

BEST CONDITION EVALUATION

RIDERS NAME _____ REGION OF AERC _____

HORSES NAME _____ DATE _____

FINISHING TIME _____ FINISHING PLACE _____ RIDERS WEIGHT _____

*'The Riders finishing weight is determined immediately at the conclusion of
the ride, without tack, and with the same clothes that were worn during the ride.*

COMMENTS from pre-ride inspection, or from observations during the ride: _____

A. VETERINARY SCORE SHEET

A. Veterinary Evaluation *(Max. 100 pts.)*   SCORE

1. **Pulse:** *(Vet. to fill in criteria)*
   a. Up to _____ -0 points
   b. _____ to _____ -2 points
   c. _____ to _____ -4 points
   d. Greater than _____ disqualify
   *Note: Pulse criterion must be geared to
   ambient conditions and should be
   decided by Vet. Committee.*
2. **Respiration:** *(Vet. to fill in
   criterion)*
   a. Good (less than _____) -0
   b. Fair (_____ to _____) -2
   c. Poor (_____ to _____) -4
   d. Greater than _____ disqualify
3. **Hydration:**
   a. Good -0
   b. Slightly Dehydrated -2
   c. Moderate Dehydration -4
   d. Severe Dehydration-disqualify
4. **Mucus Membranes:**
   a. Normal -0
   b. Injected -2
   c. Toxic -4
5. **Capillary Refill:**
   a. 0 - 3 seconds -0
   b. 3 - 5 seconds - 2
   c. 5 seconds or more - 4
6. **Gut Sounds**
   a. Normal -0
   b. Slightly Diminished -2
   c. Poor -4
   d. Colicky—disqualify

                              Subtotal _____

                                                    SCORE

7. **Muscle Soreness and/or Back Pain:**
   a. Normal -0
   b. Slightly -2
   c. Mod. Soreness -4
   d. Severe soreness or
      tieing up — disqualify.
8. **Locomotion:**
   (def. of "Lameness")
      "Being off")
   a. Perfectly sound -0
   b. "Off" sl. leg weary -3
   c. Markedly "Off" -4
   d. Lame-disqualify
9. **Joints, Tendons, & Ligaments:**
   a. Normal -0
   b. Slight Filling or
      Swelling -3
   c. Severe Filling -6
   d. Severe injury to this
      area—disqualify
10. **Open Sores and Galls:**
    a. None
    b. Slight w/no impair-
       ment of function -3
    c. Sores w/impairment of
       function—disqualify
11. **Attitude, Willingness and
    Coordination:**
    a. Exceptional -0
    b. Acceptable -5
    c. Fair -10
    d. Poor—disqualify

                              Subtotal _____

                    TOTAL VET SCORE _____

B. TIME FACTOR *(Maximum of 100 Points Awarded to the Fastest Rider)*

Fastest Time for Winner of the Ride _____ Automatically Awarded 100 Points = _____

Finishing Time of Contestant _____ Subtract 1 point for every minute behind winner _____

                    TOTAL SCORE IN TIME FACTOR CATEGORY _____

C. WEIGHT FACTOR *(Maximum of 100 Points Awarded to Heaviest Rider of Contending Horses)*

Weight of Heaviest Rider of Contending Horses_____ Automatically Awarded 100 Points _____

Finishing Weight of Contestant_____ Subtract 1 point for every pound less than winner _____

                    TOTAL SCORE IN WEIGHT FACTOR CATEGORY _____

Head Veterinarian _____   **TOTAL FOR ALL THREE CATEGORY'S** _____
                                                              (Max. of 300 Points)
Ride Manager_____ NAME OF RIDE_____

(This Scoresheet must accompany AERC Ride Results for Winner to be eligible for Regional and National Awards Program.)

(Mail Original Copy to AERC with Ride Results. Second copy to Ride Manager. Third Copy to Rider)

D: Ride Checklist

EVERY HORSEMAN has a different idea of what he should take to an endurance ride, but this list will give you some ideas. It's a very good idea to use a checklist in packing so that you don't forget something essential.

Two nylon halters (always carry a spare)
Two strong lead ropes
Lead rope with chain if needed
Shipping wraps or boots
Sheet
Cooler (optional)
Lined blanket for use at night
Vet wraps or track bandages with wraps
Grooming tools and products (brush, scraper, hoof pick, sponge, scoop, etc.)
Ice boots and ice chest (if using ice to cool)
Fly spray
Stethoscope and thermometer
Equine first-aid kit
Leather punch and leather thongs for repairs
Wire cutters
Feed tub
Water buckets
Hay net
Salt block
Grain and hay
Electrolytes, and wormer syringe to administer
Supplement

Shovel
Water hose
Saddle
Two bridles (again, have a spare)
Two sets of pads and girth covers
Spare set of reins
Spare cinch or girth
Spare stirrup leathers
Breast collar
Easyboot
Spare set of horseshoes
Flashlight
Banana bag or other small saddle bag
Knife
Electrician's tape (good for solving small problems)
Registration papers
Ride information
Health certificate for interstate travel
Camp chairs

Depending on whether you are roughing it or traveling with a camper, make up your own list of personal items to take along. See the what to wear section in Chapter 5 for the proper clothing to pack.

Bibliography

THE FOLLOWING books discuss horse care and training in an informative, accurate manner. Some of them do not pertain directly to endurance riding, but provide insight into the horse and his care.

ENSMINGER, M. E. *Horses and Horsemanship.* The Interstate, Danville, Ill., 1969.

GREEN, BEN. *Horse Conformation.* Northland Press, Flagstaff, Arizona, 1974.

JACKSON, NOEL. *Effective Horsemanship.* Arco Publishing Co., New York, N.Y. 1977.

MUSELER, WILHELM. *Riding Logic.* Arco Publishing Co., New York, N.Y. 1976.

PODHAJSKY, ALOIS. *Complete Training of Horse and Rider.* Doubleday, Garden City, N.Y., 1967.

———, *The Riding Teacher.* Doubleday, Garden City, N.Y., 1973.

SEUNIG, WALDEMAN. *Horsemanship.* Rev. ed. Doubleday, Garden City, N.Y., 1961.

WAGONER, DON, ED. *Conditioning to Win.* Equine Research Publications, Grapevine, Texas, 1974.

———, ED. *Feeding to Win.* Equine Research Publications, Grapevine, Texas, 1973.

———, ED. *Veterinary Treatments and Medications,* Equine Research Publications, Grapevine, Texas.

———, ED. *The Illustrated Veterinary Encyclopedia.* Equine Research Publications, Grapevine, Texas.

WILCOX, SHEILA. *The Event Horse.* Lippincott, Philadelphia and New York, 1973.

Background information for this book was derived from these books, and the following publications and papers:

AERC Endurance News. P.O. Box 1, Auburn, California 95603; issues Jan. to Dec. 1979, Jan. to May 1980.

AERC 1978 Yearbook of Endurance Riding. P.O. Box 1, Auburn, California 95603.

AERC 1979 Yearbook of Endurance Riding. P.O. Box 1, Auburn, California 95603.

HAMILTON, SAMANTHA, "Before You Saddle Up," *Equus* magazine, 656 Quince Orchard Road, Gaithersburg, Maryland 20760; September 1978.

Trail Blazer. Susan Gibson, ed. P.O. Box 1855, Paso Robles, California 93446; issues Jan. to Dec. 1979, Feb. to May 1980.

Index